*"I like the emphasis on finding one's own structure, and on enabling teen-agers to develop goal-setting and time-management skills. It provides a tool-box which students can use to build structures that are meaningful to them."*

Amanda Hyldahl
The Home Schooler Newsletter
Meadville, PA.

*"Beverly puts it all together in a student directed time management program that begins with goal setting, defines terms such as credit, grade, syllabus, etc. and then helps them choose their necessary courses geared to their future plans. She shows how courses can be formatted with the traditional approach, modified approach, unit study approach, or an independent approach."*

Vicki Goodchild
HIS Publishing Co.
Ft. Lauderdale, FL.

*"I'm impressed with this book for several reasons, but primarily because this is the first high school handbook I've seen that is addressed to the high school student rather than the parents. The subtitle of the book is: A Time Management, Organization, and Career Exploration Course for Christian Home Schooled Teens and it truly is."*

Paige Smith
Live & Learn - Home School Newsletter
Humboldt , CA

*"Very well thought through. Lots of great ideas. It will give them (home schooled teens) a systematic and thorough means of preparing and checklisting their high school years."*
Claudia Joye
Chester County (PA) Homeschoolers

*"I like the binder system. It keeps my subjects organized. I don't have to flip through a lot of papers. My English doesn't get mixed up with my Math and I can switch from subject to subject easily."*
Joseph Shipley, 15
Seattle, WA

*"A complete course on goal setting, planning, and time management. Unlike other manuals, the intended audience of this handbook is primarily the teenage homeschooler. Information about and ideas for every subject required for a high school education at home are presented. Students are given instruction for creating their own courses and forms are provided to help develop a portfolio."*
Vicky Jensen
Learning Lights
Eugene, Oregon

*"This guide helps students save a lot of time by creating a high school 'plan.' It helps with the most practical particulars of individual courses, projects and even daily and weekly scheduling. The college prep section is invaluable. I recommend* Home School, High School, and Beyond *to all secondary students and their parents."*
Janice M. Hedin
HSA Community Liaison
Maple Valley, WA

*"In my opinion, this manual should be on the shelf of every home schooling family. Beverly L. Adams-Gordon has laid a wonderful foundation for home schooling the high schooler."*
Jacqueline Clark
Christian Home Educators Network
Maryland

# 3RD EDITION

# HOME SCHOOL, HIGH SCHOOL, AND BEYOND ...

A Time Management, Career Exploration, Organization, and Study Skills Course

## In This Program You Will Learn To:

### Manage your time and energy by:
Setting goals and establishing priorities
Using your time and talents for God's Glory
Organizing your school records & study areas

### Plan and prepare for college by:
Planning and documenting every course you take
Completing high school graduation requirements
Developing a plan for financing your higher education

### Prepare for Career and Vocation by:
Seeking God's will for your life
Exploring career and vocational options
Selecting post-high school education

By Beverly L. Adams-Gordon
Illustrated by Angelina J. Sylvester

iii

Castlemoyle Books
15436 42nd Avenue South
Seattle, Washington 98188
206/439-0248

3rd Edition:

First Printing
9 8 7 6 5 4 3 2 1

The author has attempted to provide as accurate and universally correct information as is possible in this text. Where regulations and procedures are particularly subject to change or variations, suggestions of how and where to verify the information are provided. However, because every state's rules and regulations regarding home schooling are different and subject to changing legislation, it is not possible to cover all of the possible variations. Therefore, you should check with your own state's home school support group, or the higher level institution you will be attending regarding graduation and other legal requirements to verify the procedures and activities you set up through this course. The author, publisher, and its agents will not be held liable for any damages incurred due to inaccurate information or misapplication of the information contained in this book beyond the retail purchase price of the book.

Printed in the United States of America

## Publisher's Cataloging in Publication
(Prepared by Quality Books Inc.)

Adams-Gordon, Beverly L.

Home school, high school, and beyond —: a time management, career exploration, organization, and study skills course/ by Beverly L. Adams-Gordon; illustrated by Angelina J. Sylvester. — 3rd ed.
p. cm.
Includes bibliographical references and index.
ISBN: 1-888827-15-7

1. Home schooling — Handbooks, manuals, etc. 2. Christian education — Handbooks, manuals, etc. I Title.
LC40.A43 1996 649'.68'0973

QBI96-20449
LCN:96-085082

"God has given each of you some special abilities: be sure to use them to help each other, passing on to others God's many, kinds of blessings.",

1 Peter 4:10

Dedicated

To

My Mother

Elsie Ann Adams

"List Maker Supreme"

## Acknowledgments

No book can be written without the support, cooperation, and encouragement of many people. The third edition of *Home School, High School, and Beyond* is no exception to this rule. First, I would like to thank my patient, talented husband who spent hours helping me make this new edition an improvement. I also would like to thank Anna Shipley, my assistant, for her hours of proofreading and candid suggestions. And finally I would like to thank the families who have used the previous editions for their constructive criticism and warm praise of the earlier editions.

Beverly L. Adams-Gordon

v

# PREFACE TO PARENTS

This book is written with the goal of helping your high school student take a more active role in his own education. Written as a nine-week high school course (Occupational Education credits), the student begins with the "big picture" of exploring career options and interest areas. This exploration will help the student determine what he needs as far as post high school education and, therefore, high school courses. With your help, he can then plan individual courses and proceed to using time-management tools on a weekly and daily basis.

The entire processes' focus is on the student's obligation and accountability to God for the stewardship of his time and talents. This approach helps the student to begin to own his education. Making it something he has done and chosen for himself (by seeking God's will), not something "done to him" or imposed upon him by his parents.

There are nine sections in the book, each comprising about one week's work. Following each section are activities ("exercises") designed to get your student started using time-management and organizational tools. These assignments require increasing involvement in the planning and documenting of the courses and activities the student pursues. This process serves two purposes: 1) the student learns and makes a habit of using life-long organizational tools and skills and 2) allows him to gradually increase his involvement in the decisions regarding his education.

The type of assignments and exercises used in the text make a teacher's answer key impossible. The work the student will do are far too individual in nature. Therefore, it is highly recommended that the parent(s) take the time to read through the text before assigning it to the student. This will help prepare you for your student's questions and to assist him with the various projects. It will also help you determine if the student is progressing through the text appropriately.

Most assignments build on others, therefore you should make sure your student completes each exercise. Some of these assignments are of an on-going nature (such as exploring career options or using a weekly planner). Once the student has begun such activities he may go on to the next section. You should check to make sure he is continuing his efforts on earlier assignments, however.

To complete the assignments in this course, your student will need the following items: one 2 " three-ring binder; extra-wide, seven-tab index dividers; tabbed month dividers; a 1" binder for each course (you'll need approximately six of these, which will be reused as you begin new courses, so choose sturdy ones); 9x12" manila envelopes (one for each course  approximately 24); and at least one copy of each form found in Appendix E. 1 Providing all the materials and copies at the beginning of the course will avoid delays in progress (and excuses).

Guiding and assisting your son or daughter through this course will not only help you establish a framework for home schooling through the high school years, it will help you establish a new, adult-to-adult relationship with your child.

I hope you enjoy watching your student grow and bloom. God bless your family as you start this exciting new "ed-venture."

Beverly L. Adams-Gordon

Author

---

1 Some parents prefer to also provide a separate 1" binder for ``academic'' records (instead of keeping them in the student's planner). This keeps them neat and safe. This separate binder can also be useful for storing other records, such as achievement test results. When you read through the book, you will want to make a decision regarding this.

# CONTENTS

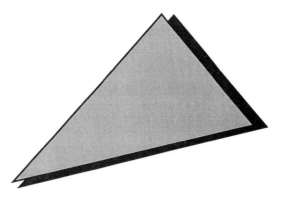

# Welcome to High School!

This program is for high school students, especially those who are home schooled or are in individualized education programs, just like you. As a high school student you are ready to take on more responsibility for your life. Learning to take charge of your life is an awesome challenge, but it is one only you can tackle for it is you that is ultimately responsible to God for how you live your life.

This book will help you meet that challenge. Working with your parents or a teacher who cares about you, you will learn the skills you need to make the most out of your life and to be a good steward of the time, talents and gifts God has given you. It will guide you through the process of getting your high school education and preparing for your future by teaching you the value and importance of setting goals.

With your parents' or teacher's help, you will lay the groundwork for your future by becoming a goal setter and achiever. You will learn to use your time effectively with a time-management tool designed especially for high school students, but modeled after the type of calendar you are likely to use as an adult.

Goal setting and managing your time effectively are a matter of establishing habits. As you work through this program, remember that it takes time to develop habits and that learning new skills always begins with a bit of fumbling around. Your first attempts at developing schedules and plans may not be perfect, they may even fail. But keep on trying. Think about how many times you fell trying to learn to ride a bike and remember that you kept getting back on because you wanted to learn to ride. If you begin all your efforts with this same type of perseverance, you are sure to succeed and to develop the habit of good stewardship!

God Bless you as you take your first steps towards your adult life.

Beverly L. Adams-Gordon

Author

# Exercises

Completing these exercises is the first step on your way to the challenge of your lifetime: to make the most of the time and the talents God has lent you.

## Exercise I

Get a good start to this program by making it yours. You will want to obtain a large 2 1/2", three-ring binder; one set of month (tabbed) dividers; and a set of seven-tab index dividers (you'll learn more about this as you go through the book.) You will also need copies of many of the forms. To begin with, you will need at least one copy of each form (most are two-sided). You may copy the other forms as they are referred to or you may print the number suggested in the introduction of the forms section (Appendix E). You will want to three-hole punch all of your forms.

## Exercise II

Once you have your forms copied, three-hole punch them and insert them into your binder. Your first section, using the tabbed dividers, should be labeled Academic Records. Behind this tab insert your Personal Data Sheet. You should complete the Personal Data Sheet with the help of your parents. Label the second section "Calendar." Behind it place your month dividers. The seventh section of your binder should be labeled Extra Forms. Behind this section store all the other forms you had copied until directed to use them.

# Establishing Goals and Setting Priorities

*Before you can learn to manage your time*

*effectively you have to establish your priorities.*

*Goals are one type of priority that will help you*

*plan the best use of your time. In this section you*

*will learn about goals and goal setting.*

# Goals Give You Purpose

For many people, just looking at their long term goals or big projects is overwhelming. They do not know where to begin, so they do nothing. Others lack focus, so they spend a lot of time on things they later discover are unimportant to them and they don't accomplish what really matters. All too often they become bogged down in trivial things and loose track of the priority tasks and the things that really matter. Suddenly, it's too late, and they realize they have not completed an important task on time or have failed to do the things that are most important to them.

Without a goal in mind or at least a vision of your future, you will not make the most out of your high school years. More importantly, you will not make the most out of your life. Not making the most of your life would be a great sin, because our Lord made you to love and serve Him. And we should always strive to do that to the best of our God-given capacity.

Setting goals for your future will help motivate you to do your best work today. It will give you purpose for all the courses you may take,

even if it is only so you can get that diploma or get into college. You will know why you are taking every course you are taking. Each course, even those you dislike, becomes a part of your plan, not a plan imposed on you by someone else, but your plan.

## Three Types of Goals

There are basically three types of goals: long-term goals, intermediate goals, and short-term goals. The long-term goals are the "What I am I going to be when I grow up" type. Most cover dreams for ten to twenty years from now. But they can be shorter or longer depending on your age and the goal itself. Intermediate goals are the goals you hope to achieve in the next couple of years. An example of an intermediate goal might be "to graduate from high-school." Short-term goals, are goals you hope to reach relatively soon say in three months, such as "to finish this semester with all A's."

## Break Down Your Goals

Every goal you set, long term or short term, usually can be broken down into a series of shorter steps or tasks. Let's look at an example of both a long term goal and a short term goal, broken down into smaller steps.

A Long Term Goal: "To become a doctor"
• Complete an Internship
• Graduate from medical school
• Get into medical school
• Get into college/university
• Graduate from high-school
• Take  AP Biology  course

A Short Term Goal: "Complete science research paper on time (by 3/20/99)"
• Task 1: Select topic (3/2)
• Task 2: Research & note taking (3/10)
• Task 3: Make an outline (3/11)
• Task 4: Write a rough draft (3/14)
• Task 5: Proofread & edit draft (3/15)
• Task 6: Write final draft (3/16)
• Task 7: Someone else proofread (3/17)
• Task 8: Type final draft (3/18)
• Task 9: Submit to teacher (3/20)

*Setting goals begins with God.*

As you can see, the goal "to become a doctor" can be broken down into a series of steps just as easily as the goal "To complete my science research paper on time." You also probably noticed you can work from the future down, as the example of "to become a doctor" or you can work from a first-things-first approach, as in the example of the research paper. It does not really matter which direction you work, as long as you break down the goal into smaller units.

You may also have noticed that a goal can have specific deadlines. These deadlines can help you schedule your time and efforts. Planning specific due dates for each of the tasks of a project such as a research paper will help you meet your goals.

## Goals Begin With God

The first step to goal setting is to pray for God's direction in your life and to thank Him for the gifts and talents He has given you. It is important to remember, when you ask God for direction in your life not to expect a light to suddenly come on or a voice to boom down from Heaven telling you what to do or how to do it. It could happen, of course, but God tends to lead us in subtler ways. We must be open and receptive to the opportunities God puts before us.

After you have asked for God's direction in your life, and you have made yourself open to His gentle hand, you are ready to begin building your future, step by step, goal by goal.

# Setting Your Long Term Goals

You may already have a very clear picture of what you want out of life or "what you want to be." You may already have decided on a career. If you have, you are a fortunate young person. God has already revealed a fraction of His plan for you. But for most young people, with a whole world of choices, it is a little less clear. Your parents and grandparents, the people who love you and care the most about you, are there to help you with this task. Your pastor, a caring teacher, or another adult that cares about you may also be willing to give you guidance with this task. Go to them and talk to them about the possibilities for your life. Ask them at what they think you would be good.

Sometimes, others can see our potential better than we can. Inquire about how they decided the direction of their own life. What they would do if they had it to do all over again? Don't be afraid to do this, your elders are flattered when you seek their help. It shows them you respect their wisdom and experience.

If, after talking to people who know you well and whom you respect, you still really are not sure what you would be good at, there are professionals that can help. Career counselors can be consulted at your local high-school or community college, usually at no cost. Many of these professionals have available Interest and Skill Surveys (tests that you cannot fail!) that can help you get a realistic picture of your options. Most community colleges provide these tests free or for a small fee.

*Thinking about career choices can help you select high school classes.*

A computer software program, Career Path, is now available to the home market. This program provides interest profiles as well as a directory of careers. It is published by OnTrack Media and retails for approximately $79.98. While these tests will not tell you what to do with your life, they do reveal interest areas and suggest careers that are related to them. With that information you can find out what the different careers in your interest area require, as far as education and skills, and then you can begin investigating these options.

If in the investigations mentioned above you only narrow down your "search" for your future to "I know I want to work outside" or "Whatever I do, I know it must involve children," or even "All I know is I will need lots of contact with people," you have come a long way toward making career choices. Some students, for instance, know that they like Science. Knowing this, they can look for careers that use a Science background. Such information can help you identify possibilities, as well as eliminate possibilities. They can also help you make educational decisions while you are still trying to identify your options.

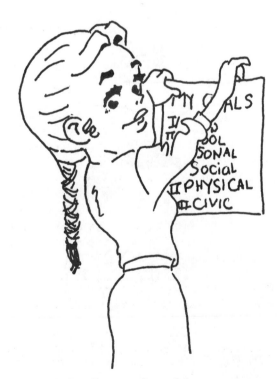

*Set goals for all areas of your life.*

## Investigate Career Options

There are many ways to investigate career options. One way is to read about them. You will find the public library has shelves of books on career options. Most of these books are excellently written and give the details on the education required, talents needed, what type of salary you would expect, working conditions, etc. Another way is to talk to people who do the type of work you are investigating. Many people find your interest in something that is dear to them flattering. You should assume their career is important to them or they probably would not continue in it. Visiting businesses that do the type of work you think you would like is another good way to meet such people. You should also let your family and friends know what you are considering. They may know someone in that field you can talk to and who is willing to help you.

As you narrow down your choices, you may want to consider volunteering your services or getting a job at a place that does similar work. You might also investigate organizations for young people considering particular careers, such as the Boy Scouts Police Explorers. While you most likely will not be able to practice the tasks involved in the actual career of your choice, you will get to know people who do that type of work. You will also get a feel for the type of environment you would be working in if you entered the career permanently.

## Prepare for all Possibilities

Making your career choice is probably one of the most important tasks of your life. It should be thought out prayerfully and carefully. While exploring your options you will need to be preparing the groundwork for any possibility. You should assume that your plans will include college, until you have definitely decided otherwise. Too many young people have not done this only to decide in their Senior Year that they need to go to college. Then they discover they have not taken the courses required for admission. This is expensive and frustrating, so it is best to assume you will go on to college until you are sure otherwise.

## Set Goals For Whole Life

Too many people use goal setting only in the academic and professional areas of their lives. As a Christian, you need to look beyond this narrow, worldly view of success and life. You should make it a habit to set goals and schedule time for the other priorities in your life. If you fail to do this, two things could happen. First, you are likely to resent your plan and not follow it. Second, if you follow your plan, you are likely to regret not having done some of the things that are important to you.

I have met too many people who have gotten caught-up in the "(worldly) success is all important" trap. Too often they discover their children grown, their parents gone, their marriage lifeless, and their spiritual life withered. All the money and all the prestige in the world is little comfort without loved ones with which to share it. As you are working on your goals, think about all the areas of your life. The planning pages included in this course have goal setting sections for the following areas of your life:

**Spiritual:** Setting goals for your spiritual growth should be your first priority.

**Academic:** Most of the text of this course is geared to planning for your academic activities and setting your academic goals.

**Personal/Financial:** This is where you set goals and allow time to take care of yourself, schedule your errands, your shopping, clean your bedroom, or do your laundry. For some students this is also the place to schedule and plan your work or money making sources.

**Social:** Use this area to set goals of visiting friends, writing to relatives, planning a party, or spending time helping a younger brother or sister learn a new skill. If you plan your play-time, you can control it and it will not disrupt your study time.

**Physical:** All of your goals will be worthless if your body falls apart. Use this area to set goals for healthier living and getting enough exercise.

**Civic:** Set goals for yourself to be involved in your community. Write letters to the editor about issues important to you. Volunteer your services, or plan any other activity you feel will make your town, state, country, or world a better place to live.

---

## How To Make Your Goals Achievable

1. Ask for God's direction in your life. Remember that the first stage of any goal setting process is to seek God's direction and then to remain open to His gentle hand.

2. Be realistic about your expectations. As students, an improved understanding of a subject you have little aptitude for is preferable to getting hopelessly bogged down if total mastery of the subject is just not in the cards. Likewise, when planning career decisions, it pays to know your strengths and weaknesses as well as your favorite and least favorite activities.

3. Be realistic when you set goals. Do not aim too high or too low and do not be particularly concerned when (not if) you have to make adjustments along the way. You can be overly realistic, too ready to sigh and give up just because something "is not in the cards." There is a fine line between aiming too high and feeling miserable when you do not come close, aiming too low and never achieving your potential, and finding the path that is right for you.

4. Concentrate on areas that offer the best chance for improvement. Unexpected success can do wonders for your confidence and might make it possible for you to achieve more than you thought in other areas.

5. Monitor your achievements and keep resetting your goals. Daily, weekly, monthly, yearly ask yourself how you have done and where you would like to go now.

# Exercises

## Exercise III

Set goals for each of the priority areas of your life, for each of the time periods listed on the copy you made of the Life Goals Sheet. Use your Imagination — Dream a little. If you have not decided on a career goal, just close your eyes and imagine your life at each of the time periods. The shorter term goals should be easier for you, but try to come up with a goal for each time period. Save your Life Goals Sheet behind your personal data sheet in your binder.

Remember: As you begin goal setting, don't be afraid to change your goals as you go along. In fact, to emphasize this point you may wish to write all of your goals in pencil. This way you will be less timid about changing them. You may seriously consider a number of careers as you continue to investigate. Or your mid-range goals may change as you decide on a different path leading to the same long-range goal. The short-range goals will undoubtedly change, even daily.

**Dates to Remember**
Birthdays and Anniversaries

## Exercise IV

Make one of your first goals to complete this program and to make a habit of using its organizing and time management tools. To do this you will need to make sure you allow time in your schedule for it. To schedule something you need a calendar — as a home schooler you need a calendar designed for your special needs. To create such a calendar, label the second section of your five-tab dividers "calendar." Behind the divider, insert the copies (from your extra forms section) of the Dates to Remember/Commemorative Days sheet, the four Academic Year Calendars, and the tabbed monthly divider sheets. On the Dates to Remember sheet, record the birthdays and anniversaries of all the people about whom you care.

Now, take out 12 copies of the Month Of _____ (calendar pages) sheets. Look at this year's calendar and starting with this month fill in the dates for each month. Now look at the Commemorative Days & Holidays sheet and record the holidays for each month. Do the same for the information recorded on your Dates to Remember form. Insert each month's calendar

Life Goal Planning Sheet

page behind the appropriate month's tabbed divider.

Look at each month and choose a date each month to go over your goals. Many students choose a date near the end of the month as this will get you off to a smooth start for the next month. The dates you choose are not as important as planning for them and sticking to your plan. Write down this goal for each month on your calendar pages. Adjust your date if it falls on a holiday or another day you are not likely to follow your plan. This will eliminate a potential failure. Insert your pages behind the monthly dividers. Congratulations! You have taken your first step to managing your time.

## Exercise Va

If you have not selected a career goal, start working on it. Make your next goal to "select a career goal." Break this goal down into smaller steps — plan and schedule time to follow the steps and follow your plan.

## Exercise Vb.

If you have selected a career goal, your next step is to plan what steps you will take after high school to get there. Do you need college? Vocational School? Job Training? Make your next goal to "select after high-school training." Break this goal down into steps and schedule time to follow the steps and follow your plan.

Note: Exercise V is an assignment that you should consider an on-going activity. You should not wait to have completely finished this exercise to go on to the next section. After you have completed Exercise Va you should come back and begin working on exercise Vb. In later sections you will be given more information which will possibly help with these steps as well.

| Sunday | Monday | Tuesday | Wednesday | Thursday | Friday | Saturday |
|--------|--------|---------|-----------|----------|--------|----------|
|        |        |         |           |          |        |          |
|        |        |         |           |          |        |          |
|        |        |         |           |          |        |          |
|        |        |         |           |          |        |          |
|        |        |         |           |          |        |          |

© 1995 Castlemoyle Books

**SECTION 2**

# Create Your Tentative High School Plan

*While you continue to make your career choices and long range goals, reality insists that you also live today. You need to set some intermediate goals. One intermediate goal that almost all young people have is to complete high school. In this section we will look at what is required to achieve this goal. When you are finished with this section you will be able to complete your Tentative High School Plan.*

# High School Has Its Own Terminology

Before you begin, you must have an understanding of the terms used in this planner so that you do not become confused. When the term subject is used, it refers to the general categories of learning such as English, Science, Mathematics, and so on. When the term course is used, it refers to some type of division of the subject. Biology is a course in the subject area of Science. A unit is a narrower division of a course or subject. For instance, using the Science example again, you could take a course in Biology. Within the Biology course you can devote one unit to Botany, which is the study of plants .

## You Earn Credit For Work

In high school and college, you earn credit for the work you do in each subject, as well as marks or grades. A student earns credit for a unit of work. Your credits tell how much work you have done. The grade or mark is the score you have earned. It shows the quality of the work you have done. This system tells colleges or future employers both how much and what quality of work you have done.

Credit can be awarded in a variety of units. For this text we will use the definitions provided by the State of Washington's Department of Public Instruction for high schools (which is fairly standard across the country). According to the state, one credit equals 180 hours (50 minute hours, the length of a standard high school class period) of instruction plus approximately 72 hours of homework. This equals 222 hours of effort for the student. For home schooled students, actual time may be shorter as the "hours of instruction" are one-on-one and therefore are more concentrated.

Generally speaking, a textbook is designed for a full year and is equal to one credit of work. You can count the completion of a textbook and all its assignments as one credit. You must be cautious however, as some books are designed for half-year and others for quarter-long courses. Additionally, some textbooks are designed as two-year courses. Consult the teacher's manual of the textbook you are using to be sure. If you are using college textbooks for some of your courses, you will earn more than one high school credit for the work. Likewise, if you are using a book designed for younger students you should not give yourself full high school credit for the completion of the work. Students using these types of textbooks, the "Project," or "Contract" method for their education must use hours to compute their credits.

If you are using the "Project" or "Contract" method, you should also consult standard textbooks as to topics generally covered in a course to make sure you have covered all the topics expected for high school level of instruction.

## Grades Show the Quality of Your Work

When you receive a grade in a course it tells the quality of the work you have done in that course. Colleges and employers are generally most interested in how you have done on the average. To calculate this "average," you simply add the numerical value of each grade (see below) and divide by the total number of credits earned. The resulting total is called the "grade point average." Grade point averages are derived from the following weights of grades:

| | |
|---|---|
| A = 4.0 - 3.71 | A- = 3.7 - 3.31 |
| B+ = 3.3 - 3.01 | B = 3.0 - 2.69 |
| B- = 2.7 - 2.31 | C+ = 2.3 - 2.01 |
| C = 2.0 - 1.71 | C- = 1.7 - 1.31 |
| D+ = 1.3 - 1.01 | D = 1.00 - .75 |
| D- = .75 -.25 | F = 0.0 |

# Creating Your School Calendar

The standard school year in the United States is 180 days in length. Most textbooks are designed for courses to cover the "year" of work. The school year is often broken down into smaller units or terms. By dividing up the year you can achieve greater flexibility and variety in your course selections. The year can be divided into quarters, semesters, trimesters or mini-units.

The semester is the most common division of the school year. A semester is equal to half a year of work or one-half high school credit. It equals 111 hours of work for most students.

The quarter system of awarding credit is the most flexible and the most manageable. The quarter is equal to one quarter of a year of work or one-quarter high school credit. It equals about 56 hours of work for most students.

The advantage of the quarter system is that you can actually complete five quarters during the calendar year with small breaks between quarters. This allows you complete your high school education early or if you are behind to catch up to your age-mates and graduate at the standard age. With this system you would study nine weeks, then take one week off. This leaves an additional two weeks to be used on other legal holidays and at Christmas and Easter.

Another advantage is that you have the greatest flexibility in scheduling your elective-type classes. For instance, under the subject of health you can take one-quarter of first aid, one-quarter of Anatomy and Physiology, one-quarter of nutrition, and one-quarter of child development. This works with any number of subjects and makes the "unit" approach most manageable.

The trimester is the least common and hardest to use for computing credit, yet it may be just right for you. A trimester divides the year into three equal units of approximately 75 hours each. Some home school families use this method along with three vacations of about five weeks each. One vacation is generally taken at Christmas time, another around Easter, and the third during August.

The mini-unit is another very flexible method that some home school families find effective. A mini-unit covers two weeks effort of approximately eighteen hours each. A credit in a subject would require 18 mini-units. Likewise, a half credit would require nine mini-units. This system allows you to "school" year-round with two-week or one week breaks at your discretion. Schooling year-round, using the mini-units method, allows you to complete the equivalent of one and one-half credits in as many (6 to 10 subjects is typical) subjects as you are pursuing per year.

Some students use a combination of the above methods for scheduling their school work. If you attend a regular school or use a correspondence program you will be required to use the method the school dictates. Home schoolers and their parents need to make a decision about which system or combination of systems they will use. The yearly Tentative High School Plan forms (masters in back of this book) are designed for ease in planning either full year, semester, or quarterly systems.

*You need to establish your calendar and credit requirements.*

# What Grade Are You In?

Home schoolers are often asked "What grade are you in?" A simple question that for many home schoolers has not been easy to answer, since often they are working on several grade levels, depending upon the subject. Now that you are in high school it will be easier. High School consists of four "school years" which are referred to as either grades or classes. In "grade" terms these would be your 9th, 10th, 11th and 12th grades. Each grade is also referred to by a formal name as follows: 9th graders are called Freshmen, 10th graders are called Sophomores, 11th graders are called Juniors, and 12th graders are called Seniors.

The year you are a Freshmen is referred to as your Freshmen year, and so on with each year. All the students in a school who are in the same grade or year are called the class. For instance all of the 10th graders or Sophomores make up the Sophomore class. The term class is also used to denote the year you expect to graduate. If you will graduate in 1998 you are a member of the Class of '98. (If you will graduate in the year 2000 you will be called the "Class of Double-Ought.")

Most high schoolers need between 19 and 24 credits to graduate. (Information on decid-

ing which is most appropriate for you is discussed later in this text.) After you and your parents have determined how many credits you need to graduate, you simply divide the number by four. When you finish that number of credits you have completed a "school year" and move up to the next grade.

It works something like this: If you need 24 credits to graduate, while you are working on your first six high school credits you can say you are a ninth grader or Freshman. Once you have earned six credits and while you are working on the next six you can say you are a 10th grader or Sophomore, and so on.

One word of caution, while it may be exciting to be in a higher grade than your age mates you may not wish to publicize your "grade." You may also find it to your advantage to not actually graduate early. In some states, students who have not graduated, but are academically ready for college, can attend Community College or Junior College at no cost. In Washington State the program is called Running Start. With this program you earn both college and high school credit. More information about this type of program is given later in this text.

# What Do You Need To Study In High School?

```
┌─────────────────────────────────────────┐
│                                           │
│  Minimum Graduation Requirements          │
│                                           │
│      Subject                  Credits     │
│      English                     3        │
│      Math                        2        │
│      Science                     2        │
│      Social Studies              2.5      │
│          State History & Gov.     .5      │
│          U.S. History             1       │
│          Contemporary World History,      │
│          Geography & Problems     1       │
│      Occupational Education       1       │
│      Health & Physical Education  2       │
│      Fine Arts                    1       │
│      Electives                   5.5      │
│      Total Credits               19       │
│                                           │
└─────────────────────────────────────────┘
```

Now that you understand the ways in which a high school education can be divided, you must decide what subjects to study and how much time is needed for each subject. First, you must consider the state requirements for receiving a high school diploma. Then, you must consider where you are going after high school. 121212You need to meet both sets of criteria if you are to make the most efficient use of your high school years. You should begin by mapping out the minimum state requirements on your Tentative High School Plan. On this page is the list of the minimum requirements for Washington State students (WAC 180-51).

(Note: The requirements you must meet are those which are in effect at the time you begin grade nine. Any changes which occur after this time only affect future students. It often happens that an older brother or sister may have a different set of requirements than his younger brother or sister.)

As you look over the required courses for a diploma in Washington State, you may be surprised at the number of credits required. Most local school districts also have minimum requirements and so more credits are needed for graduation than listed above. If you attend a private or public school (or plan to complete your senior year at one), you should consult the student handbook. It will explain which courses are required for graduation from your school. If you live in a state other than Washington you should consult your state home school association for information. (See Appendix D for addresses and phone numbers.) Home schooled students should also consult with their parents regarding minimum requirements.

If you are not beginning this program at the start of your ninth grade year, you should begin by filling in the Tentative High School Plan with the courses you have already completed with a passing grade. Then finish by filling in classes you must complete to earn a high school diploma.

## College Bound Students Need Advanced Preparation

Students planning to attend college will find the minimums listed above are nowhere near sufficient to qualify for admission to most universities or four year college. Again, if you have not yet decided on a tentative career goal, make your high school plans as if you will be attending college. There is no real harm in taking extra or more demanding courses, but to be unprepared can be costly and time consuming. You will want to avoid having to take any high school level course at college, since you must pay for every course. On this page is a general recommendation of a typical course of study for college bound students.

### TENTATIVE HIGH SCHOOL PLAN
Use Pencil to Complete

| | 9th | 10th |
|---|---|---|
| English | | |
| Mathematics | | |
| Social Studies | | |
| Science | | |
| Health and Physical Education | | |
| Occupational Education | | |
| Fine Arts Credit | | |
| Foreign Language | | |
| Electives | | |

© 1995 Castlemoyle Books

### TENTATIVE HIGH SCHOOL PLAN
Use Pencil to Complete

| 11th | 12th | |
|---|---|---|
| | | English |
| | | Mathematics |
| | | Social Studies |
| | | Science |
| | | Health and Physical Education |
| | | Occupational Education |
| | | Fine Arts Credit |
| | | Foreign Language |
| | | Electives |

© 1995 Castlemoyle Books

This list is only a generalization and may not be adequate for some colleges. It is best to refer to college books or to a college admission counselor if you have selected a specific college you may attend. If you plan to attend vocational school or seek on-the-job-training, you should see counselors in regard to recommended courses of study for these options.

Planning which courses you will take in high school is another area where an adult who has "been there" can be helpful. Ask him if he had to do it over again what would he have studied. Ask him what high school courses helped the most in his line of work. Also ask about what colleges he went to and why or why not you should consider them. You should try to make it a point to make a "mentor" of an adult who is active in the careers you are considering. Remember, most adults are flattered by the attention and sincerely want to assist young people to be successful.

You should visit the schools you think you would like to attend as soon as you identify them. Consult these schools about which subjects you need to study in high school in order to qualify for admission. The earlier you seek this type of guidance the better. Some colleges, especially small private colleges, make their selection based as much on a student's character as on past academic performance. Showing that you think ahead, are persistent, and that you prepare in advance are good indicators that you will make a good student.

## Creating A Good Balance

It is a rare individual who is superior, even good, in every subject. If you are, count your blessings. Most students are a little better in one subject or another. Some students simply like one subject more than another — and do not think that does not change your attitude toward it. Others are naturally gifted in one area and only average in others.

Unfortunately, you cannot just take the courses you are good at or that you like and ignore those that are difficult and that you dis-

---

# College-Prep Requirements

English  4 years, college prep, honors or AP recommended
Math  Algebra, Geometry, Trigonometry, & Pre-Calculus
Science  Two years lab science required (Biology, Chemistry, and physics recommended)
Foreign Language  2 years required; 3 or 4 years recommended
Social Studies  3 years
Occupational Education  1 year
Health/P.E.  2 years
Fine Arts  1 year
Academic Elective  1 year minimum

## Suggested Course Schedules For College-Prep Students

| Freshmen (9th) | Sophomores (10th) | Juniors (11th) | Seniors (12th) |
|---|---|---|---|
| English | English | English | A.P. or Honors English |
| Algebra | Geometry | Algebra II with Trig | Pre-Calculus/Calculus |
| Foreign Language | Foreign Language | United States History | Contemporary World |
| State History(1/2 year) | World History or elective | Foreign Language | Problems/Civics |
| P.E./Health | P.E./Health | Chemistry or Physics | Foreign Language |
| Earth Science | Biological Science | Occupational Ed. | Chemistry or Physics |
| Elective (1/2 year) | | | Fine Art |

like. The law or the college's admissions policies dictate that you pursue what they consider a well-rounded course of study.

As you think through your high school schedule, keep in mind your areas of strength, weaknesses, and interests. Attempt to schedule your classes in a balanced way. For instance, try not to schedule all subjects that are difficult for you in the same term or year. Break up your plans so that you always are pursuing at least some classes that are easier or more interesting to you. Keeping this balance within your week or even your day as well as the quarter or year is also helpful to most students.

## Be Prepared to Adjust Your Plans

In addition to your Tentative High School Plan you will find Academic Year Plan sheets in this program. These forms are designed to allow you to evaluate your progress toward your goal at the end of each term, quarter, and/or year. This allows you to reevaluate your plan as your goals change or become more definite. Remember that putting your plan on paper is to guide you, not to lock you on one path for life. It is not unusual for people your age to change their life goals a number of times before settling on their "life vocation." While it is advisable to reevaluate your plans on a regular basis, each term is sufficient for reevaluating your course goals. It is important that once you decide to begin a course that you complete it. Never fall into the trap of completing half of a course. You will spend a lot of time getting nowhere, which is not the purpose of this program.

**Life Rule**: Plan every course and project you undertake and finish every course or project you begin.

The spacing on the Academic Year Planning Sheet also allows you to be more detailed in your proposed program. For example, on your Tentative High School Plan you may have indicated the goal to take four years of English courses. On your Academic Year Planning Sheet you can be more specific. You can divide each of your English courses into four quarter-long units each year (e.g. grammar, creative writing, drama, and report writing). This concept is more applicable to home school students, who often have more flexibility in how they pursue their studies, than it is to students in institutional, correspondence, or satellite schools. If you opt to follow this idea you will find the list of course topics and potential course titles for each of the basic subject categories found in Appendix A helpful.

The course handbooks (course syllabus) provided to entering high school students (or from your local community college for that matter) are also very helpful in this way. You will find in these a wealth of ideas on topics you can study within a category of courses as well as descriptions of the content (often referred to as the scope and sequence) of many courses. Most public high schools will give you a copy of their course syllabus or student handbook. All you have to do is ask for it.

*Maintaining a good balance of the type of courses you take at the same time is important.*

# Exercises

## Exercise VI:

a) Home schooled students: With your parents, establish your own school calendar. Decide if you will operate on a mini-unit, quarter, semester, or yearly basis. Will you work year round, have summers off, or do school work four days a week year round? What is required to earn a credit as far as number of hours, etc.? Record your decisions so there is no question about them later. Store your decisions behind your Life Goal Sheet in the Academic Records section of your binder.

b) If you attend an institutional, correspondence, or satellite school you will not have the freedom to make these decisions with your parents, but should find out the policies of the school you will be attending so that you can use it to help you plan your calendar later.

## Exercise VII:

Using the decisions you made for Exercise VI plan this school year's overall schedule. Record the days you plan to take as vacations and holidays on your monthly planning sheets. Make sure you have scheduled time each month to review your plans and goals. You should have a schedule which allows for a minimum of 180 instructional days or the minimum for your state.

## Exercise VIII:

a) Complete a tentative high-school plan as described in this section. Store the completed document in the Academic Records section of your binder.

b) Evaluate yourself: What are your strengths and weaknesses? What skills do you need to accomplish to prepare for college? How do you want to spend your free time? Have you included provisions for these in your plans?

# SECTION 3

## Working Out This Year's Plan

In the last sections you were introduced to some of the terminology used to describe high school activities, such as subject, course, credits, and terms. Following this work, you were assigned to work with your parents to plan your school calendar and create a tentative high school plan. In this section, using your school schedule and your tentative high school plan, you will decide which courses you will take this year .

# Mapping Out Course Schedules

Most high school students study six courses each school term. This allows them to earn six credits each year, for a total of twenty-four credits in four years. This usually requires six hours (50 minute) plus homework time each day. Classroom teachers generally plan for an hour or two a week for most subjects. While this is the traditional approach, you may find that you will learn better working in a different manner. For instance, some home schoolers like to arrange their morning plans to study about one hour of Math and maybe an hour of English, the remaining four hours or so are spent doing short concentrated units on varying topics. Other home school students like to arrange their courses into smaller units. For instance, instead of taking a standard English book and beginning at page one and giving themselves a credit when they reach the end of the book, they focus on topics like Short Story Writing for nine or ten weeks. When you are home schooled you have many options. However to take full advantage of this freedom you have to thoroughly understand the credit accounting system.

## Credit Accounting System

The easiest way to think of how to calculate credits and the time required to complete them is to think in terms of the equations shown in the figures below. The equation assumes the following: 180 days is the traditional number of days in a school year (D); 50 minutes is a typical class session (M); and a typical teacher will assign homework which will require approximately 72 hours to complete (H). (However, some courses, such as P.E., require little or no homework time.)

If you were to read this equation you would have 180 days times 50 minutes, divided by 60 minutes, plus 72 hours homework equals 222 hours or the average number of "real" hours needed to earn one high school credit (labeled C). The sum (C) can be divided by a variety of time units or T (e.g. 180 days), to give a total number of hours per unit of time (H). So, if you

$$\frac{180 \times 50}{60} + 72 = 222$$

$$\frac{D \times M}{60} + H = C$$

$$\frac{C}{T} = H$$

want to know how many hours per day you need to receive one credit during the first half of the school year, you could divide 222 (C) by 90 days (T) which equals approximately two and a half hours per day (H). In this way the total number of hours per credit can be divided into a number of still smaller units. These smaller units can then be added together in a variety of ways to equal a full (one) credit. Some of the popular options for breaking down credits are as below:

Full Credit  222 hours
       1-36 week-long session = 1 credit
Half Credit  111 hours
       2-18 week-long sessions = 1 credit
Third Credit  74 hours
       3-12 week-long sessions = 1 credit
Quarter Credit   55.5 hours
       4-9 week-long sessions = 1 credit
Unit credit  12.5 hours
       18-2 week-long sessions = 1 credit
       9 2 week-long sessions = 1/2 credit

Using these units, you can easily determine how many days or weeks you need to work on a subject to earn a credit or a portion of a credit. The advantage of such knowledge allows you to record credit hours for some unique activities. For instance, one student enrolled in a local ski school. The ski school met every Saturday during the ski season between 9 a.m. and 11 a.m. (2 hours). Following the lessons, students could use ski lifts and the school's equipment until 2 p.m. (3 hours). The student usually practiced his skiing two of these hours, giving him two additional hours of skiing each week. Since the ski class met for twelve weeks he was able to count 48 hours toward a P.E. credit needed to graduate. For a course such as P.E., which usually does not require homework, this is an adequate number of hours to count as one-quarter credit.

Keeping track of hours or time is not the only way to determine when you have earned a credit. Most home schoolers consider that they have earned a credit, in Mathematics for instance, when they reach the end of the book. This can be a good system too, but you must be careful that the book is intended as a full year course for students at your level. You must also be sure to take all of the necessary tests and quizzes which would normally be taken "in school."

Another method which works well is setting a goal for a certain level of proficiency or knowledge. This system is excellent in such skill courses as typing. Some families believe that if the student can pass the final exam which accompanies the text with a certain percentage score (say 85%) they know enough to say they earned a credit. If you plan to use such an accounting method, you should check the acceptability of your criteria for credit with any institution you plan on attending later, or from which you plan to receive your high school diploma, in advance if at all possible.

# Selecting the Actual Courses

When you created your tentative high school plan, you mapped out which subjects and how many credits you needed to earn each year for the next four years. Now you are ready to decide the actual courses and the content of those courses (See Appendix A for topic suggestions for courses under each of the basic subjects). For many home educated high schoolers, choosing the courses you will take and their

content requires nothing more than picking out the appropriate course texts. Some home schoolers will use textbook courses in mathematics and use their interests and talents to outline many of their other courses. For others it means creating the course for themselves. You may be somewhere in the middle.

When traditional high schools (or the organization issuing your diploma) and college admissions directors evaluate your portfolio, the main criteria most often used to judge it is "equivalency" to the traditional program. The easiest way to make sure your courses are "equivalent" is to examine the scope and sequence or learning objectives for the courses the local high school offers which are similar to what you plan to study. Many school districts are willing to provide this material to home schoolers. You may also find such information in a number of books available from your local home school supplier. *The Home School Manual* by Theodore E. Wade, Jr. is currently one of the only such books which lists information on home schooling high schoolers.

*You can earn credit for unique activities.*

Alternate ways in which you can determine this information would be to examine the teacher's edition of a textbook for the course. You can also get a pretty good idea of the typical content of a course by examining the brief description provided in high school course catalogs. These are available to students at most local high schools for free. You should be able to acquire one by just asking. If you have selected a specific college you wish to attend you should contact them regarding their entrance requirements for home schoolers.

Knowledge of the information you are expected to know at the end of a course or the course's "scope and sequence" can help you select the appropriate textbooks as well as to create alternative learning experiences. If you are pursuing a course which is not normally taught at the high school level, you may create a list of the things you hope to learn by the end of the course. This list is called your learning goals. With this list of "goals" or "learning objectives" you can be sure your program meets the equivalency criteria expected by schools you may later attend. You will learn more about creating your own courses in the next section.

# Home Schooling Can Be Formatted In Many Ways

Let's take a look at four typical, home schooled ninth graders to see how some of the different options for formatting a home school high school program might look. All four students are trying to complete the college-bound suggestion listed in Section II of this book. All need to take one credit each in Earth Science,

State History, English, Algebra I, and Foreign Language, and one-half credit each in Health and P.E.

## Jordan's Traditional Approach

Jordan's family likes a very traditional approach to schooling. For them, this means the typical school textbook for most subjects. Most of the books are purchased from popular Christian textbook companies. His mother purchases for him the English, Health, Mathematics, Science, and Spanish books from their catalogs. Since the publishers do not offer Washington State History (which he is required to have in order to graduate) his mother purchases a textbook from a local home school store. He will only complete half of the Health book this year (saving the rest for next year). For his P.E. credit he plans to take a weekly Karate class throughout the year.

Jordan plans his weeks and days around the program laid out for him. To do this he has taken the number of pages in each textbook and divides them by 180 (the normal number of school days). This lets him know how many pages he should complete in each course, each day. Every day Jordan makes sure that he completes "one-day's worth" of school work. Some days it only takes Jordan three hours to do all his school work. Other days he needs seven hours. Jordan has recorded in his calendar specific checkpoints so he can be sure

*Jordan plans his schooling well in advance.*

*Jerry uses park programs for P.E.*

not to miss any deadlines. For instance he has scheduled all his unit tests for science for specific days. If he finishes a unit of science before his deadline he takes several days to review as preparation for the test. The school year ends, for Jordan, when he has finished all of the assignments in his books. Since Jordan would like to graduate early, he often does more than a "days worth" of school work.

## Jerry Uses a Modified Approach

Jerry plans to use the "four, nine-week long quarters" formats for his calendar. The first thing Jerry puts on his schedule is P.E., since he plans to join the park department's football team this fall and the baseball team in the spring. These two sports will give him adequate hours for his one-half credit of P.E.

For the Health credit he plans to take a Red Cross First Aid and CPR Class and to take a quarter-long course in Human Anatomy using library resources and the *Atlas of Human Anatomy*.

His parents have decided that he should take Latin as his foreign language. They enrolled him as a part-time student for this course at a local private High School. He and his parents

selected the *Key to Algebra Series* for his math, knowing that when the course is completed he will have the equivalent of a full year of Algebra.

For his Earth Science credit, he decides to a use quarter-long topical units. He decides to complete a unit on the *"Geology of Oregon,"* using a book by the same title for his text during the first quarter. The second quarter he plans a unit on weather and climate with an emphasis on the Northwest. The third quarter he focuses on Astronomy for which he plans several trips to the local science center's observatory. For his fourth quarter he plans to do a unit on Oceanography, which will tie in with his family's vacation at the beach.

Jerry and his mother plan to combine his History and at least some of his English this year. He plans to study research and report writing as he studies the history of the state. Part of his English credit will be earned through Literature.

## Julia's Family Uses Unit Study

Julia and her family take a completely different approach to her schedule. Like the boys, Julia plans to attend a four year college but her schedule is nothing like Jordan's or Jerry's. The majority of her day will be spent working on *Project Discovery: The Pacific Northwest* a unit study program, along with her brothers and sisters. This program, which has lists of

*Julia completes "unit studies" with her family.*

objectives and lesson plan ideas for various age groups, is designed for a family learning together. Through this program Julia will earn her credits for Pacific Northwest History, Earth Science, English and Literature. She will also earn her P.E. credits through family activities, many related to the Unit Study. The only subjects not pursued as a family are Julia's Mathematics, Foreign Language, and Health. Julia has decided she would like to learn American Sign Language for her foreign Language since there are a number of deaf teens who attend her church. She has been given permission to take a sign language course through the local community college's non-credit extension program. For Health she plans a half year study of Nutrition. For Mathematics she plans to complete the *Merrill Algebra I* text.

## Jennifer Plans Her Own Courses

Jennifer is what is known as an autodidact. She likes to be completely responsible for her own education. Her parents encourage her and support her efforts. Jennifer knows she learns best by doing, so she uses very few textbooks. Equipped with the learning objectives for each of the courses she must complete, she and her mother outline activities that will help her mas-

*Jennifer takes CPR for Health credit.*

ter the objectives. For Science she has builds a home weather station, visits an archaeological dig, stays up late to study the stars and visiting observatories. For History she is visits museums, watches historical movies and documentaries, and reads journals. For a unit on Government she decides to do a time-line project to trace how home schooling legislation was passed in her state. She also plans to volunteer as a Senate Page during the legislative session. Since she enjoys baby-sitting she signs up for a Red Cross First-Aid & CPR class as well as a baby-sitting class. Then she volunteers as an aid at a pre-school for developmentally delayed children.

For her P.E. credit she plans to work with an aerobics tape three times per week throughout the year. She earns half of her English credit by selecting books to read from the *High Schooler's Classic Reading List* and half by documenting her studies and writing reports. Her mother gives her grammar assignments by determining, from her writing, her most frequent errors. She studies Japanese using the Living Language Series tapes and by watching a Japanese language course on public TV each week. She also watches the local Japanese TV station and has invited a Japanese exchange student to stay with her family. The only textbook she plans to use is *Saxon Algebra I.*

## The Choice is Yours

As you can see, each of these students took a completely different approach to home school studies. Each family and/or student has found what works best for them, yet each family has accomplished the same end result. The most important requirement is that what you study is "equivalent" to traditional programs. That means you need to make sure that upon completion of a course that you have learned the same basic knowledge, not necessarily that you have learned it in the same way. Several precautions must be taken in this area. First, make sure that any institution you plan to attend later or which will issue your diploma agrees with your idea of "equivalent." Talk to any colleges you are considering early and keep up annual communication (policies change recently they have become more liberal).

Another consideration in planning is the sequential nature of some subjects. Mathematics and Science, for instance, are very closely aligned and sequenced in traditional high schools. At the high school level, Science courses generally require increasing levels of Mathematics. It can be quite difficult to succeed in Chemistry, for instance if you have not completed Algebra I. Likewise, Physics without some background of Geometry will be more difficult.

If you live in an uncooperative school district, plan to attend an uncooperative college or live in a state with difficult home school laws, you may need to enlist the aid of a home school extension school or a supervising teacher. Your local home school organization should be able to help you locate such assistance. You may also find the resources listed in Appendix D

helpful. The main thing, and I repeat **the main thing**, is not to wait until the end of your Senior Year to work out how you will get into college or be issued a diploma! You must plan ahead and keep up with changing legislation.

# Keep Your Days Varied

Do not take all courses that are hard for you or that are not your favorite subjects at the same time. Plan so your subjects have a good mix! God gave you gifts and talents as well as challenges, referred to by some as crosses to bear. You should keep these things in mind when you plan the courses you will take. For instance, if you find Science a challenge you should not plan on taking two courses at one time. Likewise, if you are a fanatic for Art type course you should try to pursue at least one during each term.

---

### Freshman Year Plan
(Use Pencil to Complete)

| | 9th |
|---|---|
| English | |
| Mathematics | |
| Social Studies | |
| Science | |
| Health and Physical Education | |
| Occupational Education | |
| Fine Arts Credit | |
| Foreign Language | |
| Electives | |

© 1995 Castlemoyle Books

---

### Checklist for 12th Grade

The following activities should be done during 12th grade (about age 17). Twelfth grade career planning activities should be started as early as possible during the fall. This planning is extremely important, especially for the college-bound student. Review this list when you register for courses and check when completed.

**For All Students:**

☐ I have reviewed and checked my planning sheet.
☐ I have reviewed the credits I have earned toward graduation. I have made arrangements to make-up any deficiencies that exist.
☐ I have visited with a career counselor for help in selecting a career or vocation.
☐ I have met with recruiters from all branches of the military service. (For students considering military careers.)
☐ I have applied for graduation, and ordered my cap and gown.

**For College-bound Students:**

☐ I have checked admission requirements for my choice of colleges.
☐ I have taken the college entrance exam(s) WPC, ACT, or SAT in the early fall (if not taken last spring).
☐ I have reviewed my college choices for the final selection and application and have written for out-of-state college application forms and procedures.
☐ I have made application to the college or colleges of my choice early this fall.
☐ I have made plans to attend the appropriate college information sessions.
☐ I have applied for financial aid during the month of January.
☐ I have applied for scholarships at national, state, and local levels.
☐ I have arranged to study for and take the exams for Advanced Placement Programs which will benefit me.
☐ I have researched and enrolled in appropriate early-entry college courses.

**For Students Planning Vocational/Job training:**

☐ I have made application to the community college or vocational school as soon as it was possible.
☐ I applied for financial aid during the month of January.
☐ I applied for scholarships.
☐ I am aware of the fee schedules and possible financial aid available for the school(s) I am considering.
☐ I am aware that some post-high school vocational programs require up to a two-year waiting time. I have followed the required procedures including paying the fees to get on the waiting list of the school(s) I am interested in.

© 1995 Castlemoyle Books

# Exercises

## Exercise IX:

Review the Checklist on the back of the Academic Year Form for the grade you are beginning (or are in at this time) to keep up to date on college/career planning. If you have already completed some of your high school years, look at the Checklists for early grades as well. Go over these checklists at the end of each month so that you do not miss any of the things you should accomplish.

## Exercise X:

With your parents and the suggested topic ideas found in Appendix A or a local High School's student guide select the actual courses you will take this year (or the next year if you are preparing for your first term of ninth grade.) If you did not complete this task in the last section, decide now how you will format your home school calendar and curriculum. Schedule any applicable dates (term endings) or vacations determined by your "school" calendar on your monthly planning sheets.

## Exercise XI:

Set Goals for each of the other areas of your life using the Goal Setting section of this year's Academic Year Calendar.

# SECTION 4

## Planning Individual Courses

*In the previous sections of this text you determined what subjects you need to study in order to graduate from high school and what courses you will tentatively take this year. In this section you will learn how to create and plan your own courses using a list of learning objectives. You will also learn about selecting learning resources and how to set up evaluation criteria for each of your courses.*

# Creating Your Own Course Syllabus

In addition to a plan for your school year or semester, you need a plan for each of the courses you take. This process varies in complexity from mapping out when you will study various chapters of a specific textbook to deciding which books you will study and which projects you will complete. Most home schooled, high schoolers work closely with their parents or their supervising teachers on this type of planning. However, some home schoolers leave these decisions completely to their parents and teachers, while a few plan their courses completely on their own. You should discuss with your parents (or teacher) how much and to what extent you will be involved in and expected to complete your own course planning. No matter how involved you are in the creation of your own courses you should read this entire section.

## Custom-made Course Plans

Many home schoolers find it exciting and of great educational value to explore some areas of their unique talents and interests. Knowing how to create your own courses, which will be

*Creating your own course is often necessary, especially for art and other "hands on" subjects.*

acceptable as high school credits, is especially valuable in the creative or manipulative areas where textbooks are generally not available. (Remember, you will find a list of possible topics for each subject area in Appendix A.) It is also useful to students who have a more "hands-on" learning style. Translating activities and projects into courses equivalent to those offered by institutional schools is more challenging than using the standard textbook approach, but it can be done.

"Equivalent" generally refers to content learned, not the method, materials, or even time used to learn the material. Most of your home school courses should have a similar or "equivalent" content as those pursued by students in institutional schools. This is especially true of courses such as math, science, and grammar. For history, art and elective-type courses there is more leeway and creativity allowed.

## Course Should Have a Purpose

With the above in mind, the first thing that must be determined for each of your courses is the overall purpose or aim. The overall purpose is basically a statement of what you hope to get out of the course or what you hope to learn. For instance, if you are interested in creating a pottery course you might express your overall aim or purpose something like this:

"The purpose of this pottery course is to learn more about pottery and pottery making."

After you have determined the purpose, you can establish your learning objectives. Learning objective are basically the specific skills, knowledge or attitudes you will have when you successfully complete the course. The following is an example of the objectives for the pottery course in our earlier example:

When I finish this pottery course I will:

1. Understand the basic processes required to complete a simple pot;
2. Be able to describe the basic materials

and equipment used by a potter;

3. Understand and appreciate the history and artistic style of pottery making in at least two different cultures; and

4. Have experienced the creative process of making a pot.

The purpose or overall aim you established and the list of objectives you create may at first seem redundant, but let's look at how a slightly different purpose can be translated into a different set of learning objectives.

Purpose: To learn about pottery making.
Learning Objectives:
1. I will be able to describe the steps required to make a simple pot.
2. I will be able to describe the basic materials and equipment used by a potter.
3. I will make at least one simple pot.

As you can see the simple omission of "... learn more about pottery..." changes the focus of the course from practical (hands-on) and appreciative to simply a practical course.

To recap, the first steps to planning your own course are to establish a purpose and to list the skills, understandings, and/or appreciations (attitudes) you hope to acquire through your study. The front page of the Course Planning Sheet allows space for you to record your purposes or aims and your specific learning objectives for your course. It also provides space for a basic description of the course or important background information.

Many teacher's guides and teacher's resource books list learning objectives for different courses at the high school level. As mentioned before, the course catalog or student's handbook issued by a public high school also can be a valuable aid to such planning. *The Home School Manual*, edited by Theodore E. Wade, Jr., *The Christian Home Educator's Curriculum Manual (Jr./Sen. High)* by Cathy Duffy, and *Mary Pride's Big Books of Home Learning, Vol. 4* (by Mary Pride) are three additional resources for topics and skills which are normally covered in high school. *Encyclopedia Brittanica*'s Propedia provides an outline to just about any topic about which you would want to learn.

## Textbook Course Simplify Steps

Many students use a basic textbook approach for at least some of their courses. In comparison to the above, the process of creating a course using a textbook is relatively simple, since you usually do not have to determine your own goals and objectives. Most textbook publishers have done a careful job of thinking through all of the objectives for standard courses. Therefore, all you may be required to do is to determine when you will study each unit or chapter, which exercises you will complete, and when you will take the tests which are provided in (or with) the text.

It may be tempting to take the easy way out (as described above) by using "textbook" courses exclusively for the majority of your courses, but you should use caution. It is generally a wise idea to at least check what objectives the authors of a textbook have decided are important. Then you can decide if they match your own goals and objectives. Sometimes the process will lead you to eliminate a section of the text. You will often need to add activities or search for more detailed information on a topic to accomplish the objectives you and/or your parents see as important. For in-

**Course Planning Sheet**

Name of Course: _____

Number of Credits: _____ Credit Category: _____

Date to Start: _____ Finish Date: _____

Brief Description: _____

Overall Purpose/Aim: _____

Specific Learning Objectives: _____

stance many families desire a history program that places greater emphasis on Bible History. Likewise, you may want to eliminate units which cover topics which are in opposition to your family's values or faith. Even classroom teachers make such adjustments to their "textbook courses." As a home schooler you should consider such adjustment within normal procedures.

You should also remember that most classroom teachers make assignments beyond the textbook in courses such as English, History, Literature, and Science. For instance, in high school History classes you will often be expected to complete at least one research project per semester or quarter (two to four per year). Likewise, English and Literature classes often have set requirements for outside reading, as well as writing assignments. Science classes will usually require experiments and investigations. In some instances the students are also shown films or go on field trips as part of their course work. These activities should be determined before you begin the course.

# Brainstorming Learning Resources

After you have determined why and what you wish to learn, you are ready to begin selecting the materials and resources on which you will draw. Resources for learning may include people as well as things. You may access traditional textbooks, library books, or reference books. Your learning resources may include attending organized classes or interviewing knowledgeable people.

The key to selecting the right resources is to make sure that each will contribute to at least one of the learning objectives you identified earlier. You may need to use several resources to meet this criteria. In our "pottery course" example above, it may require the student to take a park department's pottery class for the practical experience, reading a library book on pottery which includes a discussion of clays, wheels and kilns, etc., and reading the encyclopedia entry on pottery. Additional library books may be needed to learn more about the pottery of different cultures. It also may be desirable to visit a museum or art gallery to see displays of pottery.

The Course Planning Sheet provides space to record your resource ideas from six basic categories: Reference Materials, Books and Magazines, Other Media, Outside Classes and Activities, People, and Places. These categories are designed to get you thinking about some of the possibilities. They also give you a handy place to record your ideas once you have thought of them. Generally the student and parent use this form to brainstorm together. You will probably come up with more possibilities than you can use. It is ideal if at all possible to select at least one item from each category.

**Reference Materials:** This section includes standard textbooks, encyclopedia articles, and other reference type books. Most textbooks (except for Math and English) give a broad overview of fairly large topics (e.g. a single Science text may cover astronomy, geology, weather, and more). From such reading you may develop a general understanding of the topic and then

**Resources and Materials**

| Reference Materials: | Books and Magazines: |
|---|---|
| | |
| Other Media: | Outside and Ongoing Activities: |
| | |
| People: | Places: |
| | |

go on to complete readings and activities which significantly contribute to meeting your learning objectives. Often it is helpful to use more than one textbook (if they are available) as overview reading.

**Books and Magazines:** Non-textbook or "trade" books and magazine articles tend to have more detailed, up-to-date information. They also tend to be written in a more interesting style. Use your library system's computer "card catalog" to help you identify the titles which may be helpful to you. Many area library systems make it possible for you to connect to their computers from your own home. You will also find the Index of Periodicals helpful in identifying possible magazine articles which will be of help to you. In your course planning phase you may also simply want to list some general magazines (e.g. National Geographic).

**Other Media:** The term media, in this case, refers to other forms of published information, such as computer software, videos, books on tape, and other recordings. Adding media, rather than just using books and other printed material, can add excitement to your course.

If you have a computer, you should try to use it for more than just game-type activities and word processing. Today, there is a vast array of educational computer software. The first educational computer programs were mainly of the "drill" type. These, of course, still have value in helping you "learn on your own." However, so much more is now available it would be a shame to limit yourself to drill activities. Many computer programs (especially those designed for the new multimedia computers) can be used to simulate activities you would never be able to do at home. One such example is an human anatomy program which even allows you to dissect a human being! Others allow you to walk in the shoes of those from another time and/or situation, such as in the game Oregon Trail.

The Internet and the World Wide Web can also be a learning tool. Using a search engine program available on-line such as Yahoo! you can find companies, organizations, and individuals offering information about all types of subjects through their web pages. Some college sites even have their entrance requirements and course objectives listed! Internet "user groups" can put you in touch with persons with in-depth knowledge of a variety of subjects as well. There is so much available on the World Wide Web that it is an important resource to consider. However, before accessing this resource, you should discuss it with your parents. While the information on the World Wide Web is generally free, access to the computer connections often is charged by the hour. Also, there are some sites that contain information to which your parents may not wish to have you exposed.

Likewise, videos allow you to see things that time and money probably would otherwise make impossible (e.g. tour of the Louvre Museum). Most library systems have excellent selections of documentary films (usually they are listed in a separate catalog). Do not limit yourself to documentary and travel videos though. Some "fiction" can be very educational. One student studying literature watched a number of films based on classic literature after reading the books. Another watched Gone With The Wind, Glory, and Abe Lincoln Goes to Washington as part of her study of the Civil War. Most historical fiction is really quite accurate so you should not be afraid to use it. Just do not let them take the place of your regular reading.

Other media might include "books on tape" and recorded speeches. Books on tape can help you assimilate a lot more material than would be otherwise possible, since you can listen and do other activities e.g. sew, mow the lawn, or deliver your paper route. Again, the only (warning) would be not to let recordings and other media usage replace your normal reading.

Speeches recorded by the original speaker, are an excellent resource since you can hear his tone of voice and expression. Generally, these recordings are unedited allowing you to get the feeling of an actual participant in history. Unfortunately, videos often only offer excerpts of famous speeches.

College and University libraries often have extensive media selections, sometimes actual college courses on video, that you may be able to access. Check with a school near you on their media and library use policies. Also, check with friends and relatives already attending college, they may be able to locate and borrow information and materials on subjects you are studying.

**Outside Classes, Programs, and On-going Activities:** This section is where you would list possible classes (as in the park department's pottery class), educational TV programs, and other activities which you will pursue during the length of the course. When you are considering items for this category you might also check with your local 4-H programs (they do exist in cities, too). 4-H offers programs and guides in photography, nature, horticulture, home economics, and so much more. It is too valuable of a source to ignore. Other possible outside resources include credit and non-credit community college or experimental university classes, museum courses, and Scout-type organizations. You may also find that you can participate in a single class at your local public or private high school (some states allow this).

**People:** If you were taking a course in nutrition for a health credit you may include interviewing a hospital nutritionist or county extension office. When considering *People* you should remember your interviews do not need to be face to face. One student, who was taking a history course, began corresponding with the author of her major resource book. He was located in London, England. Their weekly correspondence went on long after her project was complete and the student has netted more interesting insight into research and historical study as a result.

**Places:** Generally, *Places* will include local museums, historical sites, science centers, arboretums, and so forth. Do not limit yourself to obvious choices or overlook small town museums. One student went to his town's museum and discovered, quite by accident, a wealth of information on the history of the telephone on which he was doing a report.

If you are doing historical research you may consult the National Archives Register for possibilities. The Register lists, by topic or persons, places which store primary source materials and information. Primary source materials are actual letters, documents, and photographs by the people involved or from the time period considered. These sources have materials which you would not be able to get anywhere else. You don't actually have to visit archive sites to get the information you need. Generally, you can write to them for specific information. Most small museums and achives are glad to help courteous students, however they may need to charge you for any copies they send to you. It is generally considerate to send along a self-addressed, stamped envelope to cover their return reply.

---

**Course Requirement Sheet**

Name: _____

Course Name: _____ Ref #: _____

| Order to be Completed | Project, Report or Assignment | Due Date | Est. Time Required | Date Started | Date Completed | Pts Earned |
|---|---|---|---|---|---|---|
| | | | | | | |
| | | | | | | |
| | | | | | | |
| | | | | | | |
| | | | | | | |
| | | | | | | |
| | | | | | | |
| | | | | | | |
| | | | | | | |
| | | | | | | |
| | | | | | | |
| | | | | | | |
| | | | | | | |
| | | | | | | |
| | | | | | | |
| | | | | | | |
| | | | | | | |

# Selecting Specific Assignments

After you have determined the possible resources available, you should create a list of specific assignments and their due dates. The Course Requirement Sheet is designed to help you to do this. Course requirements generally include a specific list of exercises and activities created as a result of the brainstorming you did on the Course Planning Sheet.

Assignments generally fall into five broad areas:

- Standard Exercises and Assignments,
- Reading (excluding textbooks and references for reports and projects),
- Reports, Projects and Investigations,
- Field trips, Interviews, and Activities
- Quizzes and Tests.

**Standard Exercises and Assignments:** If you are using a textbook as the "core resource" for your course, you will probably have a standard assignment which includes reading the chapter and completing the exercises which follow it, or are included in the workbook, or are presented in the lab manual. This is especially true of most Mathematics and English courses. These will probably will be written out similarly to the following:

"Read one chapter per week and complete all the problems in the vocabulary section, the odd problems in Section A, and two of the essay questions in Section B. If your score is less than 80% on the vocabulary and Section A problems, reread the chapter and complete the even problems."

Most textbooks (and the ancillary products provided with them) provide far more exercises than are needed for effective learning by the average student. For many courses, especially Mathematics and Grammar exercise-type books, it may be more appropriate to assign yourself every other problem. The remaining problems can be saved for those times when you have scored poorly (less than 80%). This allows you to seek additional assistance before completing the remaining problems.

**Reports, Projects and Investigations:** Generally a report or project should be the major focus of each term for subjects such as History, English, and Literature. Many English, Literature, History, and Science texts will provide you with ideas for research, projects, and/or experiments at the end of each chapter. You may draw on these idea sections even if you do not wish to use a traditional textbook. (Many libraries have textbooks on their shelves you can use as idea sources.) Most "Unit Study" guides have ideas which you may use for your projects and activities.

Generally, Science classes (especially those which you wish to qualify as a "lab" science) will require experiments and investigations which require approximately two hours per week. Often there is a laboratory book which provides these activities for each chapter. In some cases however you may wish to have a longer, more detailed investigation (more on the level of a science fair project) which is a major focus of the term.

*Science courses usually require lab-type work.*

Like the problem sets at the end of most chapters discussed above, there are usually more ideas given for this type of study than you can possibly complete in one year. You are not expected to do more than two to four of these ideas per term or unit. Many times you will be able to select activities specifically related to your learning style or interest areas.

**Reading/Other Media:** Most reports and projects will require you to use a number of books and reference materials other than the primary textbook. In addition, it is common for many courses to require students to read a number of related texts per quarter. In others, you may earn a specific number of points by watching videos, reading books, and so forth related to the topic, usually with a minimum number of points required. It is not unusual to be required to give written or oral reports on the books read.

**Field Trips and Outside Resources and Lessons:** Often home school students take advantage of outside classes and activities to learn things that are difficult to learn on their own or require elaborate equipment. Others find field trips add an exciting dimension to their studies. If you are using outside resources or classes you should be sure to record any assignments that the teacher gives you on the course requirement sheet as soon as you know what they are.

**Quizzes and Tests:** They come in all shapes and sizes. They can be informal conversations with your parent or supervisory teacher on the topics you have been studying or a demonstration that you have mastered the skills. Or maybe they will be more formal written exams, such as the ready-made tests which accompany many textbooks. Others will have home-made tests created using the learning objectives as a guideline. Whatever format they come in, they are a reality for most high school students. Test dates also can serve as meaningful checkpoints of accomplishing your work. You should have some sort of test at least once per term for most courses. Setting up specific dates for each quiz and test will allow you time to review prior to that date.

In many cases you will want to also establish deadlines or due dates for each activity and assignment, as well as dates for quizzes and tests. In other cases you may simply want to have achieved the learning objectives and accomplish the required activities by the end of the course. Your list of activities and due dates (if any) should be recorded on the your Course Requirement Sheet.

An illustration which continues our pottery course example might include the following:

■  Attend Parks Department pottery class each Tuesday night, between 6 and 9 p.m., until 4/23
■  Complete research report/projects on the pottery of two different cultural groups or time periods
■  Read a general book on how to create pottery and write a summary of the steps involved
■  Create a pot using hand-building techniques
■  Create a pot using wheel techniques
■  Visit an art gallery or museum pottery display

## How To Calculate
## Percentile Grades

To calculate the percentage grade from the figures (either of individual assignments or for a total term's work), you simply divide the total possible points into the total earned points. For example if during the first quarter of the school year you completed 1246 mathematics problems and correctly answered 1026 of them (or earned 1026 out of 1246 possible) you would divide 1026 into 1246 for a total percentage of 82 (or a C) for the quarter.

The following is a representative example of how percentile scores are translated into letter grades:

93% to 100% = A
85% to 92% = B
77% to 84% = C
69% to 76% = D
0% to 68% = F or E

Many home school families have established the rule that any score of less than 77% is unacceptable and they must redo their work until they achieve the higher score. Others maintain the same grade, but require all incorrect answers to be corrected (regardless of score.)

# Establishing Evaluation Criteria

## Grading and Marking

Determining what grade you should receive for the courses you outlined can be particularly difficult for most home schooled, high schoolers and their parents. Unfortunately, it must be done. Often you need to declare your grade point in order to determine your eligibility for participation in sports, clubs, and so forth. Not only must you have grades, it is very important that you be able to describe succinctly and sufficiently exactly how your grade was determined. This can aid in the college admission process. It helps because most college entrance examiners, potential employers, and others have a difficult time understanding that it is possible for a mother to give her own child a poor grade. They obviously were not home schooled!

Traditional schools often use a grading method referred to as "the curve." With this system the students are ranked in comparison to others. When you are a "class of one," such a system is impossible. This leaves two possible acceptable grading strategies for home schoolers; Pass/Fail or the Point/Percentage System.

The pass/fail system is generally a little subjective in nature. Usually the parent or student claims a passing grade when the learning objectives of the course have been met or exceeded. (Which is a good reason for establishing your objectives before you begin.) A pass/fail grade is perfect for mainly manipulative-type courses such as Art, Shop, P.E., and/or Music. These classes generally have specific activities for which the student can present a finished product or show the ability to perform a specific task, such as being able to type 40 words per minute.

A negative of the pass/fail system is that it can be seen as too subjective for many courses (such as math). Also, generally, pass/fail scores do not translate or contribute to grade point average calculations (see Section III; Create Your Tentative High School Plan).

The point system is probably the easiest system for the home schooler to work with, especially in courses such as math. Generally points are recorded in each of the basic areas of the course requirements. For example in a history course the requirements might include the areas of Textbook Exercises, Quizzes and Tests, Quarter Report or Project, and so on.

These points are then translated into percentage scores and grades (either by assignment or for the entire course). It is the normal practice of secondary schools (high schools and beyond) to "weigh" different areas of course work. For instance, it is common for simple-answer-type questions of daily assignments or tests to be "worth" fewer points than essay-type questions.

Likewise, the entire course's requirements are often "weighted." For example, it is not uncommon for math courses to count daily exercises as 25% of the grade, unit quizzes as 25% of the grade and final or term exams as 50% of the grade. Such a system places a high value on delayed recall. Similarly, History and English

*Determining specific project criteria in advance will make evaluations fairer and clearer.*

classes often place heavy emphasis on reports, projects, and writing assignments by giving more weight to these activities.

When classroom teachers record scores in their "grade books" they generally record the number of points earned out of the total possible (e.g. 86/100 or 20/25). Thus, the name "point method." These scores are usually listed in separate sections for each of the course requirements. This allows them to determine the total number of points earned in any category, out of the total possible number of points. The Course Requirement Sheet has been designed to serve as a "grade book" and assignment planning tool for each of your courses.

© 1995 Castlemoyle Books

# Evaluating Projects and Reports

Day to day exercises, for the most part, tend to be pretty straight forward as far as grading goes. Most have definite answers, either of the yes/no or specific fact variety. For this type of assignment it is easy to record the number of points earned out of the total possible points as discussed above. Reports, Projects, and Investigations, on the other hand, present a different problem. They require more advanced planning and establishing definite grading criteria.

The key to creating a fair and predictable evaluation of projects and reports is to establish definite criteria. Such criteria could list the expected length, number of references used, format of the report, and so on. A specific percentage of the total score should be established for the different areas of the report. In our sample Project-Report Grading Form, Research Quality equals 60% of the score, Quality of Presentation equals 20% of the grade, and Oral Report or Discussion with the teacher contributes to the final 20% of the grade. Each of these major headings has a number of items to be evaluated and awarded points. As you can see in our sample, "Report Writing Guidelines" contribute to only one of the total items evaluated. You may wish to use the Project-Report Grading as it is in our sample (see forms section) or adapt the idea for the specifics of your assignments or your own situation.

# How should compositions and essays be evaluated?

Compositions and essays present a similar problem for most home schoolers. The sample Essay and Composition Grading Form may be helpful in developing your own grading system. The form provides four basic areas by which composition can be judged: Content, Organization, Usage and Mechanics, and Specific Criteria. The percentage of the total score for each of these aspects of a composition is not suggested on this form. This is because the weight of each portion is dependent upon the emphasis of the assignment. If, for example, you were to write a composition for an English assignment, you would give more weight to Organization and Usage and Mechanics. However, if you are writing the essay for a History project then Content and Specific Criteria may have more weight.

**Essay and Composition Grading Form**

Name: _____ Date Completed: _____
Subject: _____ Report Number: _____

| Assignment topics and dates | 1 | 2 | 3 | 4 | 5 | 6 | 7 | 8 | 9 |
|---|---|---|---|---|---|---|---|---|---|
| **Content** | | | | | | | | | |
| Addresses the purpose of the assignment | | | | | | | | | |
| Exhibits a sense of audience | | | | | | | | | |
| Keeps to the topic | | | | | | | | | |
| Expresses originality and/or imagination | | | | | | | | | |
| Demonstrates clear ideas | | | | | | | | | |
| Uses specific details and examples | | | | | | | | | |
| Employs effective and appropriate language | | | | | | | | | |
| Includes a variety of sentence patterns | | | | | | | | | |
| **Organization** | | | | | | | | | |
| States main idea in a clear topic sentence | | | | | | | | | |
| Evokes interest in opening sentence | | | | | | | | | |
| Includes supporting sentences relating to topic | | | | | | | | | |
| Uses effective transitions | | | | | | | | | |
| Provides a sense of closure in concluding sentence/paragraph | | | | | | | | | |
| **Usage and Mechanics** | | | | | | | | | |
| Uses complete sentence structure | | | | | | | | | |
| Follows conventions of English grammar | | | | | | | | | |
| Punctuates correctly | | | | | | | | | |
| Capitalizes correctly | | | | | | | | | |
| Exhibits neatness | | | | | | | | | |
| Spells accurately | | | | | | | | | |
| **Specific Criteria** (Character development or facts presented, etc.) | | | | | | | | | |
| _____ | | | | | | | | | |
| _____ | | | | | | | | | |
| _____ | | | | | | | | | |

© 1995 Castlemoyle Books

# Exercises

## Exercise XII

Plan each of the courses you will take during the next term using the Course Planning Sheet provided. Work with your parents (or supervisory teacher) or get their approval on your plans before proceeding. You may also wish to have your plan reviewed by the organization which will issue your high school diploma.

## Exercise XIII:

After you have completed the Course Planning Sheet, select specific assignments and due dates for each of the assignments. With your parents, decide what you must do to complete each assignment. You may wish to consult a teacher's guides or course syllabuses for this information. Record these on a Course Requirement Sheet. Store these forms at the front of each of your separate 1" binders. (You may also wish to keep a copy in your Academic Records section.) Your 1" binders will be emptied at the end of each course and reused. The contents will be stored. You will learn more about the storage system in a later section.

## Exercise XIV:

At this time, it is also necessary to decide how grades will be determined for each course and their assignments. Take your time to think through your grading methods. Most of your courses will follow the same grading scheme, so once the general guides are established it is fairly easy to adapt them to each course. You will complete Project/Report Grading Forms and Essay/Composition Grading Forms as needed.

*Note: Planning your own courses and assignments takes time make sure you allow time for it in your schedule. Additionally, you may wish to go on to the next section as you continue to create the courses you will take next term.*

# SECTION 5

## Completing Assignments & Projects

*In the last section you created a list of specific assignments along with due dates for each of your courses. If you spread out all your Course Requirement Sheets, you may get the ``I'll never be able to get all this done!" feeling. This is not an unusual feeling for new high school students. In this section you will learn to estimate the amount of time required to complete assignments and learn how to break down larger reports and projects into to smaller step-by-step tasks. You'll also learn other helpful study skills.*

# Estimating Time Needed for Assignments

Now that you are in high school you will find most of your assignments have reading, either a textbook or library research or both, as a major component. The volume of required reading generally increases as you go higher in your schooling. Knowing how much of a book should be completed each day and how much time to allow to read it can help you plan effectively.

If you are using a standard textbook as the core of your course, it is pretty simple to calculate exactly how much of the text you should complete in a day in order to complete it within a given time period. As described in an earlier section, all it requires is that you divide the number of days (a full year equals 180 days, half equals 90, and quarter equals 45 days) into the number of pages the text contains. This will tell you how many pages you must complete per day. This same procedure can also be used to determine the number of chapters which must be completed per week. Of course, this calculation method will also work for library books which have specific due dates.

If you are using the daily calculations for textbook work, you may wish to subtract the num-ber of days you will be taking tests from your total number of days. Remember, caution should be exercised when making calculations as described earlier in this course.

## Estimating Reading Time

Now that you know how many pages must be read per day to complete your work on time, it is helpful to schedule time for each assignment. To do this you will need to estimate the amount of time needed for the reading portion of the assignment. To calculate your average reading and note taking speed simply read four pages of the text, noting the time you begin and end. Divide the number of minutes it took you by four and you will know the average time required per page.

You should calculate your average reading time with different types of materials, since reading rate usually varies with the type of material. For instance, your reading rate for the story you are reading for Literature will usually be much more rapid than that for a chapter in your Chemistry textbook.

In addition to a variable rate for the types of material read, reading rates can vary with mood or attitude. With this in mind, you should allow some extra time as a "fudge factor." This fudge factor is particularly important when you first begin working with your reading time calculations.

Do not worry if at first you over or under es-timate the time it takes to read a specific num-ber of pages in a textbook. You will get better as time goes by.

When scheduling time to review material for tests and quizzes you only need to allow half the amount of time which was required to ini-tially read it. But, you do need to leave room in your plans for the review.

Are you wondering how your reading rate compares with others? Do you worry that you

*Knowing your reading speed can help you plan your study time.*

do not read fast enough? If you do, most likely you should not. Most students who have reached high school level read at an adequate rate. Besides, reading rate is not the only consideration. What matters most is how much you comprehend and remember.

If you really need to know how your reading rate compares, time yourself as you read a randomly chosen 250 word selection. Now compare the time it took you to read the text with the chart below.

- Under 20 seconds  Very Fast
- 21 - 30 seconds  Fast
- 31 - 45 seconds  Average
- 46 - 60 seconds  Slow
- 61 + seconds  Very Slow

You should only worry if your reading rate falls in the Very Slow category. If this is the case, ask your parents or teacher for help. The suggestions in the list below may also be of some help. Above all, remember your reading rate will improve with practice, so keep reading.

**To increase your reading speed:**

1. Try to keep your attention focused and concentrated.

2. Do what you can to eliminate outside distractions (no radio, TV, etc.)

3. Find an uncluttered, comfortable place to read.

4. Only look up words that are required to get a clear understanding of the concept. Other words can be left to context clues.

5. Remember that you should try to grasp the overall concepts before attempting to understand every little detail.

It is important to remember that reading rate should and does vary with the type of material read. Comprehension or what you learn from your reading is the most important factor.

## Get More Out Of What You Read

To increase your reading comprehension and the retention of what you read you need a system. The letters in the word HEART stand for each step in a study system that is effective and efficient. These steps are outlined briefly for you below. Each step will be explained in more detail as you read this section.

H = How much do I already know
E = Establish a purpose for reading
A = Ask yourself questions as you study
R = Respond & Review
T = Test yourself

### H = How much do I already know?

The "H step" requires you to think about what you already know about the subject. Psychologists have shown that you will learn and retain more if new material is related to something you already know. As you think, write down the ideas that come to mind. You may wish to do this by simply jotting them down or by building a "brain storming map."

A "brainstorming map" has the advantage of recording your thoughts in an organized way. For instance, if you were just beginning a chapter, say on "Westward Expansion," you would write this topic in a circle in the middle

*Brainstorming maps help you to focus on what you already know about the subject.*

of a blank page. Off this circle you would draw lines for the different thoughts that come to your mind, such as "Oregon Trail," "California Gold," "Pony Express," and so on. You may wish to add any supporting ideas you can think of off these lines. (See the illustration on the previous page.)

## E = Establish a purpose for Reading and study

Like knowing what you want to do with your life, knowing what you hope to get out of a chapter or book will help you approach it more effectively. Establishing a purpose for studying or reading is the second step in the HEART system. It may mean reviewing your course's or the unit's learning objectives. It almost always means surveying the material to be read.

Surveying a "library type" book and a textbook are similar. Begin by reading the covers (Can you really judge a book by its cover?), then look over the table of contents and read the introduction to the text. Look through the book to get a feel for how it's organized.

*The split-page method of note-taking is an effective study tool.*

In addition to surveying the book, you will need to survey each chapter as you go. Begin by reading the introductory paragraph to the chapter. Some books also have a list of learning objectives at the beginning of the chapter. Next, skim the pages of the chapter.

As you skim pages, read all of the sub-headings and examine any illustrations, photographs or charts (read the explanations which accompany them as you examine them). Some students also find reading the first sentence of every paragraph helpful. The first sentence is most often the topic sentence. Many textbooks also have summary paragraphs at the end of chapters which are helpful to read.

Finally, read any questions that may be at the end of the chapter. Can you answer these questions? (You may wish to add any new information you learned to your "brainstorming map.") Write down the questions which you are not able to answer. Seeking the answers to these questions will be at least part of your "purpose for reading."

Following your survey make a list of any additional questions or things about which you hope to learn. You may feel more comfortable writing a general statement that begins with: "To find out..." For example, "to find out how animals develop a sense of smell."

## A = Ask Questions as you read.

To get the most out of a book you should establish a dialog with its author. You do this by asking questions as you read. You may wish to write these questions in the margin (if you own the book) or on a separate piece of paper. You can also agree or disagree with the author. Writing these types of comments is also helpful.

If you are reading a book which does not have questions at the end of the chapter you may want to ask additional questions. As you read each paragraph or section of the book, think about what you just read. Figure out what would be a good question for that section. Pretend you're playing the television game "Jeopardy."

The suggestions in this step are really completed simultaneously with the next step, but they are such an important point it needs its own reminder.

## R = Read, Record & Respond

As you read the chapter, use the split-page note-taking method. To use the split-page note-taking method, take a piece of lined notebook paper and then measure two inches from the left-hand margin and draw a line down the page. The left side provides space for you to write questions as you read. (see A step) Writing things down is important — this prevents you missing points.

After you have finished reading, you can write answers to each of your questions on the right-hand side of the page. Try to use your own words when writing answers.

## T = Test Yourself!

The final step, Test Yourself, allows you to test yourself with your questions or with the questions found at the end of the chapter. This helps you know whether you really know your stuff!

If you use the split page approach, you can simply cover the right-hand side of the page. Look at the questions and answer them aloud to yourself. Then, uncover the right-hand-side to see if you are correct.

If you are using a standard textbook and are required to answer questions as part of your assignment, you may simply want to answer the questions (without looking at your split-page notes). You can compare your answers to the notes prior to turning in the assignment if you wish.

# Taking Notes Using The Summary Method  As You Read

Writing summaries of what you have read will help you remember the main points of a chapter. Writing a summary is something like writing a book report, only in miniature. The four steps listed below will help you to write good summaries.

### Rules for Good Summaries

1. Read the paragraph and ask yourself, "what did the author tell me?"

2. If necessary, re-read the paragraph.

3. Find one sentence (the topic sentence) that gives the main idea of the paragraph.

4. In your own words, write a single sentence that combines the topic sentence with a few details that help to explain.

When your reading is interrupted, re-reading the summaries from the beginning of the chapter can help you "pick-up" where you left off. This re-reading puts you back in the same intellectual frame of mind as when you were interrupted.

In addition to helping you to initially learn the material, summary notes can be an aid to review. Reviewing summary notes, before a quiz or test, is more time efficient than re-reading the whole chapter.

*Outlining is similar to summarizing.*

## Outlining

You can also outline your material. Outlining is very similar to summarizing, perhaps easier. The following four tips should help you outline efficiently.

### Rules for Outlining

1. Keep your outlines simple.
2. Write the main ideas in your outline.
3. Add supporting details that explain your main idea.
4. Use a form like the one given in the illustration on the previous page.

Main ideas are written next to Roman numerals. Details which support the main ideas are written next to capital letters, which are indented about five spaces or one-half inch.

You should have at least two details for each main idea. If you have only one detail it can be combined into the topic sentence. Sometimes you will have additional details, which supplement the supporting details. These are indented another five spaces or one-half inch and are written next to lower case letters.

## Quick Mastery of Material

If quick-mastery is your purpose, begin by summarizing or outlining the paragraphs in the first logical section. Before you go on to the next section, re-read your one sentence summaries or outline. Then go on to the next logical section. Keep on doing this until you have read the whole selection (chapter or book). When you have finished you will thoroughly know the material.

# Planning for Other Activities and Assignments

The basic idea of calculating reading rates can be applied to other types of assignments with some adjustments. For instance, if you calculate that you need to complete two pages of Algebra per day, you can keep a record for a week or so to learn how long it generally takes you to complete them. Then, the next week, you will have a good idea of exactly how much time to allow for Math.

This concept will work for most "standard" activities. Other assignments such as report writing, essay writing, and Science investigations are a little less predictable. However, you can get an idea by keeping track of how long it takes you to complete various aspects of these activities. For instance, if you know that your history report requires you to use at least five resources, you will be able to calculate with reasonable accuracy the time needed to read and take notes from them. Additionally, after working on a number of reports you will probably be able to determine how long it takes to write an outline, rough draft, proofread and so on.

Whenever you schedule for these types of activities, leave plenty of room for error. All things being equal, you will never receive a lower grade for completing a project early, where you will almost always lose points for being late. If you do finish early, you can use the extra time for projects which are behind schedule or to fine tune those that have yet to be turned in.

The Course Requirement Sheet provides space for you to record the estimated time required to complete each assignment, as well as a space to record the start and end time for each assignment. If you use these portions of the form and refer to them when you are planning similar activities, you will be able to make better estimates in the future. The Project Planning Sheet also can be used to estimate and record time requirements for various activities.

# Planning Larger Reports and Projects

When you complete the course planning for a full term you will see that in high school (as later in college) you are generally required to juggle two or three major assignments at one time. In order to meet the deadlines which you and your parents established when your courses were planned and to keep organized you need a system. The Project Planning Sheet provided in this text is an excellent planning tool perfect for this situation.

How does the Project Planning Sheet work? As you can see, there are two main sections: Background Information (front side) and the Project Schedule (back side). The Background information helps you focus in on the details of the assignment or project. It includes such information as due dates, purposes, and required aspects of the assignment.

The Project Schedule side helps you to outline the steps that must be taken and to set definite deadlines for each. It is really just a variation of a calendar. It is set up vertically with three months running down the left-hand side, the outline of steps on the right side.

## How to Use the Sheets

The first step to planning any project is to outline the steps that must be taken or to break down each general assignment into its component parts. So, for example, in the case of an History report on The Crusades, (or any other research project for that matter) we have identified the steps as:

1. Finalize topic
2. Initial library research
3. General outline
4. Detailed library research
5. Detailed outline
6. First draft
7. Second draft and so on
8. Check spelling and proofread
9. Get someone else to proofread
10. Type final draft (if not on computer)
11. Proofread again
12. Turn in!

Next to each specific task, you should record the estimated time you think it will take to complete the task. Using this information and your final deadline you can work backwards to schedule each task. These dates and deadlines can then be transferred to your regular calendar pages. When you are working on a project you can refer back to your Project Planning Sheet for the finer details of your plan.

Many students find that the Project Planning Sheets are particularly helpful in overcoming the "I- don't- know- where- to- begin- syndrome." If mapping out the steps is the first thing you do for every major assignment, you will always know exactly where to begin.

Having listed all the activities that must be completed to finish a project is also helpful when you are bogged down in one area. Here's how they can help in this area. Let's say that you have a project of making a book shelf for your Wood Shop course. The first step would be to outline what must be done:

1. Select plans
2. Purchase supplies
3. Cut wood
4. Router shelf dadoes
5. Sand
6. Assemble
7. Finish sanding
8. Stain

If you get to step four and find that you do not have the router bit you need to make you dadoes, you can proceed to step five and get the majority of your sanding done while you wait to acquire the bit. While this is a fairly simplistic application you can get the general idea. It is generally more easily applied to report type projects. For instance, if you are hung up on one section of your report you are often able to move on to another aspect of it. Working in this manner, for many people, helps prevent them from being overwhelmed by large projects.

After you complete a project you should make notes on your planning sheet as to how well you have planned. The Planning Sheets can then be saved as a resource for your future planning needs as described above.

# Exercises

## Exercise XV

Calculate your average reading rate for a variety of reading materials (at least three). At least one of your calculations should include the amount of time needed to read and take notes.

## Exercise XVI

Make and record an estimate of the amount of time you will need to complete each assignment and task on each of your Course Requirement Sheets.

## Exercise XVII

Use the Project Planning Sheet to plan at least one of your upcoming reports, projects, experiments or investigations. Project Planning Sheets can either be filed in your "course binders" or in the third section of your planner, or both.

# SECTION 6

# Making Weekly and Daily Schedules

*So far this course has focused on ``the big picture." In this section, you will focus on the nuts and bolts of time management. Often, it is the smaller units of time – the days, hours, and minutes – that have a tendency to slip away from us if we don't monitor them closely. As you work through this section you will establish the habit of planning and scheduling your everyday activities.*

# Managing Your Time

For any time management system to work, it has to be used continually. Make an appointment with yourself at the end of each week, Sunday night is perfect, to sit down and plan for the following week. This may just be the best time you spend all week, because you will reap the benefits of it throughout the week and beyond. During this planning time you will fill in your Weekly Planning Forms and plan your days.

The first task you must complete is to record your work hours (if you have a job), scheduled classes, and any other regular appointments on your Weekly Calendar Sheets. If your weekly schedule is fairly consistent you may want to make a "master form" of it before copying your set of Weekly Calendar Sheets.

## Make Time For God

Another item you may wish to schedule at this time (before making a "master form") is your daily personal time with God. As you plan your days and weeks make sure you include time for quite reflection and prayer. Many students

do this by planning a morning offering or prayer time each day. A favorite morning offering prayer is as follows:

*"O My God, I offer Thee all my prayers, works, and sufferings today. Help me Lord, to serve you and to help my brothers and sisters to see you in my actions and deeds throughout this day. Help me Lord, also to see how I might serve Thee best. In your name I pray. Amen."*

Many students like to say the *Lord's Prayer* and other favorite prayers at the beginning of each day as well. Some families have a "family prayer time" each morning or evening. Even if your family has a "prayer time" you should plan for your own quiet time with God.

In addition to beginning the day with prayer, many students like to begin each day with Bible study or some other worthwhile spiritual reading. This is an excellent practice. Most students find that such Scripture study helps them focus on their responsibility to make the most of their time.

Making a habit of spending "quality time with God" requires you to have it on your schedule. You should block off the time you plan to spend with God on each day's calendar. Of course, making an appointment with God does not mean you can only talk to Him during those time periods.

## Scheduling Other Routines

Other morning and evening routine activities can also be marked off at this time. Morning routines may include breakfast and personal hygiene as well as time to go over your day's schedule. Evening may include cleaning your room, at least an half an hour of recreational reading, and evening prayers. Most students also have daily chores for the family that need to be included in their plans. You may also have personal chores, such as doing your own laundry, which should be included in your schedule.

Once you work out your routine activities you will know how much time to allow for them on a daily basis. If you do not know how long it re-

*Make it a habit to spend time each day in prayer.*

ally takes you to complete your various routine tasks, you should record the actual time used

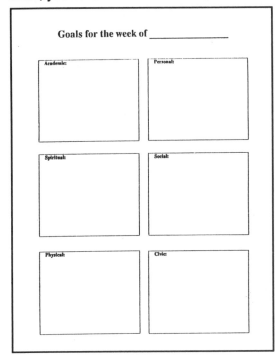

for them for an entire week. This being said, you should allow for some flexibility. Some days you may not be as efficient as on other days. If, however, the activities seem to take too long in general, see if there are ways to do them more efficiently. You may need to make a number of adjustments to the routine aspects of your schedule over several weeks. Remember, practice makes perfect when learning to manage your time.

## Setting Goals for The Week

Every week you should identify goals you wish to accomplish in each of the major life areas: Academic, Spiritual, Physical, Social, Personal, and Civic. If you set and meet one goal each week in each area of your life, you will find that you are more productive and fulfilled than the average person. Realistically, however, you will need to set more than one academic goal each week. Once you have set your week's goals you are ready to identify your week's priority tasks.

## Using Your Priority Task Sheet

The Priority Task Sheets are really nothing more than a "To Do" list. The information for this list will come from your Monthly Calendar, Course Requirement Sheets, Project Planning Sheets, Grade Checklist, Weekly Goals Sheets and any other list of tasks (such as your mom's chore chart) you have been assigned. You should add any other tasks that must be done this week: from sending a birthday present to your grandmother to doing your laundry. Once you have created your list, you can move on to the next step, putting your tasks in order of importance.

When you sit down to study (or to do any activity) without a plan, you just dive into the first project that comes to mind. Of course, there is no guarantee that the first thing that comes to mind will be the most important. The point of the weekly Priority Task Sheet is to help you arrange your tasks in order of importance. That way, even if you find yourself without enough time for everything, you can at least finish those assignments that are most important.

Ranking your "To Do" list by priority does not require you to rewrite your list. You can rank them in the column labeled priority rating. First, ask yourself this question, "If I only accomplish a few things this week, what would I want them to be?" Mark these high-priority tasks with an "H." After you have identified the "urgent" items, consider those tasks that are least important items which could wait until the following week to be done, if necessary. You may have tasks that you consider very important, but do not have to be done this week. These items might be less important this week, but are likely to be rated higher next week. These are low-priority items; mark them with an "L."

All other items fit somewhere between the critical tasks and those of low priority. Review the remaining items, and if you are sure none of them are either "H" or "L," mark them with an "M" (for middle priority).

# Filling In Your Daily Schedule

Now you are ready to transfer the items on your Priority Task Sheet to your Daily Schedule forms. Before you begin, make sure you have recorded your scheduled activities as discussed earlier. Once this is completed you will start entering your "To Do" items beginning with the "H" items first, followed by the "M" Items. Then, fit in as many of the "L" items for which you still have room.

By following this procedure, you will make sure you give the amount of time needed to your most important priorities. Block off the amount of time that you estimate you will need (see Course Requirement Sheets for assigned work). You can devote your most productive study times to your most important tasks, and plug in your lower priority items as they fit.

Besides the importance of the task and the available time you have to complete it, other factors will determine how you fit your Daily Schedules together. Some will be beyond your control: work schedules, appointments with doctors and such. But there are plenty of factors you do control, which you should consider as you put together your Daily Schedules for the week.

Schedule enough time for the task, but, particularly when working on long-term projects, not so much time that you "burn out." You quickly reach the point of diminishing returns when you try to work beyond your ability to focus on the subject. This point is different for every individual, but most students study best for blocks of about one and a half to three hours, depending on the subject. You might find history fascinating and be able to read for hours. Mathematics, on the other hand, may be a subject that you can best handle in "small bites," a half-hour to an hour at a time.

The only exception to the above would be when you are working on a major project. In such cases you may want to block out larger time periods, since you will probably will waste more time on set up if you work in smaller increments. Plan your work time in blocks, breaking up work time with short leisure activities. You will find the breaks help you think more clearly and creatively when you get back to your project.

Monday, _____

| | |
|---|---|
| 6:00 | Notes |
| 6:30 | |
| 7:00 | |
| 7:30 | |
| 8:00 | |
| 8:30 | |
| 9:00 | |
| 9:30 | |
| 10:00 | |
| 10:30 | |
| 11:00 | |
| 11:30 | |
| 12 Noon | |
| 12:30 | |
| 1:00 | |
| 1:30 | |
| 2:00 | |
| 2:30 | |
| 3:00 | |
| 3:30 | |
| 4:00 | |
| 4:30 | |
| 5:00 | |
| 5:30 | |
| 6:00 | |
| 6:30 | |
| 7:00 | |
| 7:30 | |
| 8:00 | |
| 8:30 | |
| 9:00 | |

Copyright (c) 1992, Beverly L. Adams-Gordon

# Getting the Most out of Every Day

In a previous section you were advised against taking all courses that are hard for you or that are not your favorite at the same time. This same consideration must be made in your daily and weekly plans. If Mathematics is your weak point and you do not find Social Studies particularly inspiring, do not schedule them back-to-back. Study a course you find easier or more enjoyable (these two things seem to go together) in between the two harder subjects. Better yet, plan one of these types of subjects after each of your more challenging courses when arranging your days. There are always going to be things in life that you have to do whether you really want to or not. The idea here is not to avoid the unpleasant but to arrange the day or week so that you always have something for which to look forward.

## Your Study Time

As a home educated high schooler you should get in the habit of having specific "school time." This is especially true if you plan to go on to some sort of formal "post high school" training. Your "school" time should take up the better part of your day! Your school work and related learning activities will most likely take between four to six hours per day. Remember, getting an education is the "work" of people your age.

While you will be blocking off a fairly big chunk of your day for "school," as a home schooler you have more control over which chunk you devote to it. You should plan the study hours which are best for you, if you are able to choose your own schedule. If you are a morning person, try to schedule your concentrated study and learning hours in the morning. Schedule your less strenuous activities and outside recreation and so forth during the afternoon when peak concentration is not needed. You will want to do just the opposite, on the other hand, if you happen to be a night person.

## Taking breaks

Plan your day so that you have time to stretch and relax between subjects or courses. Even with such a plan you may want to take additional breaks now and again. There is nothing wrong with taking such breaks whenever you feel you need to keep yourself sharp and maximize your quality of study. That is, just as long as the breaks are not every five minutes and do not last longer than the study period.

If you have trouble concentrating for long periods of time, you should try to increase your study periods and concentration gradually through practice. You should make it a goal to study and concentrate for one hour periods. Many students learn to do this by setting goals for themselves and giving themselves little rewards.

"Today, I am going to try to really concentrate on my Algebra for an half-hour before taking a break. If I can do that, I will reward my-

*You should set goals on a yearly, monthly, weekly, and even daily basis.*

self with 10 minutes playing a computer game before I go back to my studies."

It may seem a little funny to bribe yourself at first but, it really does work for most students. Try to think of it as giving yourself something to look forward to when you complete a task that is difficult for you.

Taking these breaks helps your study time to remain productive. Other ideas which seem to help students achieve peak performance during their study time include making sure that you get enough sleep each night, making sure you follow a good nutritional plan (do not skip meals), and that you get enough physical exercise each day. In addition to helping you study more effectively, these things are essential to the maintenance of a healthy body. Remember, your body is the Temple of God.

## To Be Efficient, Be Prepared

One way to make the most efficient use of your time is to be prepared for efficient study times. This is best done by making sure you have the supplies you need and a place to do the work. Having ready access to the supplies commonly needed for studying (see list) is a real time-saver. Keeping these items in a specific place saves you an enormous amount of time because you are not constantly having to search for them when you need them.

Having a specific study space, with a desk, lamp, bookshelf and bulletin board of your own, is the ideal. Such a space offers you a place to organize and store all of your supplies. Unfortunately, rarely does real life meet all ideals and you may not have such a place. For many home schoolers sharing the dining table with a number of brothers and sisters is reality. Such a situation does not necessarily mean you can not be organized and prepared for efficient study time. You can create a "moveable locker" using a purchased milk crate file box or even a cardboard box. The milk crate file box can accommodate "pendaflex" or hanging file folders, providing you a space to neatly store your work. You can also keep your books in the box. A pencil box or zipper bags kept within the box can be used to store for the smaller items, such as pencils, paper clips, and so on. Such a movable locker can be brought to the kitchen table during study times and then repacked and stowed in the bottom of a closet when not in use. They also travel to libraries and on vacations well!

If even finding a space at the dining room table is a challenge --it takes more space to study than to eat -- a card table or wooden TV tray may be used. These two items offer the advantage that they can be set up anywhere, even outside on a lovely Spring day.

## Use your Daily Schedule Daily

Each night (or in the morning before your day begins) look at your schedule for the upcoming day. How much free time is there? Are there "surprise" tasks that are not on your schedule but need to be? Are there conflicts you were not aware of at the beginning of the week? By checking your Daily Schedule daily, you will be able to respond to these changes.

*Taking breaks 'to play" helps keep you sharp and maximizes concentration.*

# Exercises

## Exercise XIX

Map out your basic weekly schedule. If you have set appointments, classes, or a work schedule enter them on your daily schedule for the up-coming month. Select a day and/or a time to go over your week's schedule in advance (Sunday evening is usually the best). Enter this scheduling appointment on each of your weekly calendars for the remainder of the year.

## Exercise XVIII:

Map out what you imagine your typical day should be like. Make sure you have included time for God and a daily appointment to go over your calendar. This will be a basic guide to follow. Follow this plan at least a week and evaluate how it works for you. Make any adjustments you may feel are necessary.

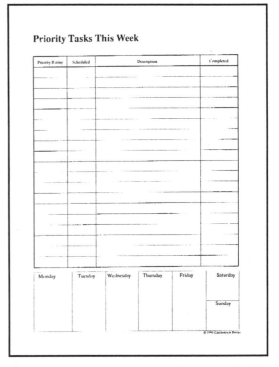

## Materials You Will Need

The following items are things you will use on a regular basis as a high schooler. If possible, you should try to own each of these things personally.

Dictionary
Thesaurus/Synonym Finder
Pencils
Erasers
Pens
Library Card
Calculator
Course Texts
Ruler
Protractor

Compass
Paper Clips
Highlighters
White-out
Glue/glue Stick
Scissors
Colored Pencils
Lined Paper
Blank Paper
Stapler & Staples
Pencil Sharpener

The following are items that are nice to have access to at home, but can easily be shared with the rest of the family:

Computer or typewriter (CD Roms offer many educational programs)
Encyclopedia set (even if it's old)
Tape recorder (for foreign language courses and note taking practice.
VCR for educational videos and foreign languages
Personal desk or study area.
Bulletin board and thumb tacks.

**SECTION 7**

# Keep Records of Your Accomplishments

*In the previous sections you have planned and
scheduled a variety of courses and worked out
your daily time management plan. In this section
you will learn how to organize, file, and maintain
your own high school records. With this information you will be able to create your own high school
portfolio and a "transcript." You will use these
records to help Admissions Directors determine if
you are ready for their programs and courses.*

# Creating Your High School Portfolio

Providing colleges with a profile of all work and a record of your learning achievements is important. As a home schooler you will need more documentation of your work than students who attend institutional schools. Therefore, you should keep a representative sample of your work or a portfolio of your work. Samples of daily work, all special projects and reports, and all tests should be saved as a record of the work completed.

An excellent system for saving such examples of work, in an organized way, is to store them in 9 x 12" manila envelopes (referred to as "Course envelopes"). Each envelope should be labeled and referenced to a Course Record Sheet that summarizes the course. These will be described and illustrated in more detail on the next page.

Large envelopes are more effective than file folders because items will not slide out of the side and work is better protected from age and yellowing in a sealed envelope. Most school work and reports will fit in this size envelope. Large projects, such as art, sewing, or science projects, can be recorded with photographs quite effectively.

Most students will find one envelope per course sufficient. However, a few courses need more than one envelope. If you need more than one envelope, each envelope should be labeled and referenced to the Course Record Sheet. Marking them as being envelope 1 of 2 and so on is also helpful. A copy of the Course Requirement Sheet, Project Planning Sheet, and any other forms specifically related to the course should also be saved in the Course Envelope.

The envelope system also is an excellent way to preserve calendar pages as records of work. By storing calendar pages as the month is completed your planner does not become unwieldy and you have backup reference of work and progress.

Some states, school districts, or supervisory teachers require the maintenance of attendance records. If you are required to keep a tally of hours and days of study the saved calendar pages can be used as documentation. You may also find the Attendance Form provided in Appendix E, (Forms Master) useful.

Your calendars can also be useful when you are planning projects similar to past projects. You can refer to your old calendars to get an idea of how long it really takes you to complete a task. You may also find storing copies of Project Planning Sheets together in a separate envelope or binder section helpful for this purpose.

---

**Course Record #\_\_\_\_**

Course: _____ Credits: \_\_\_\_ Grade: \_\_\_\_

Subject: _____ Date Begun: _____ Finished: _____

Course Description: _____

Main Textbook /Resources Used: _____ Copyright Year: \_\_\_

Publisher: _____

ISBN: _____ Text Level: _____

Comments: _____

Grading Method: _____

© 1995 Castlemoyle Books

# Creating A High School Transcript

A number of forms have been included in this planning guide to help you easily organize and collect the information colleges and future employers will most likely ask for, as well as forms that assist you in preparing for college. Keeping up to date with your record keeping, using these forms or forms of your own creation, will prevent a mad dash to organize it for your college admissions interviews at the end of your Senior Year. Each of the forms provided for this purpose is explained below.

## Academic Records

These forms will provide you with your own "official transcript" for college application. Among the forms, designed for both your and your parents' use, you will find the following:

### Course Record

The Course Record provides a complete summary of the courses you undertake. Each Course Record has a number to allow you to cross reference to your "course envelopes" and your Transcript/Report Card (described below). The beginning section states the name of the course, the credits earned, the final grade, the subject it fits under (e.g. History) and the date began and finished. You should complete a Course Record for every course for which you claim credit. Some courses may require a course record for each semester or quarter if you work on a theme basis. Students using theme units may find that one Course Record sheet will explain a number of credits that are related. If this is the case you must document the number of credits awarded in each area.

Some of the information required on this form may seem to be a duplication of the course planning sheet. But, remember, the planning sheet is designed to record ideas that you may pursue, where the course record sheet is a record of what you actually did while working on the course.

Some home schoolers find it helpful to include a photocopy of the Course Record with

the sample work. A brief description of each of the areas of this form follows:

**1. Course Description:** Make a brief, yet complete, description of the purpose and scope of the course. Again, high school catalogs are excellent resources for both describing courses taken and for determining what topics are considered basic for coverage in the courses. If you cannot find a good example for a course you are documenting you will find that a summary of the textbook's Table of Contents or a listing of unit topics sufficient at least to describe the course's scope.

**2. Main Textbook/Resources Used:** You should complete as much of the information requested in this section as you can. College entrance counselors want to know that the books you have used are from reputable publishers and that they are current enough to the subject to be accurate. The comments section allows you to describe the text. You may find the textbook catalog descriptions of texts or the

*Keeping up-to-date with record keeping can save a lot of work later.*

summary of the text provided in the teacher's edition helpful here. If you have not used a standard text, you should explain what resources were used in the comments section. Some home school students may find that they need more space when listing the resources used if they use more than one text or other creative learning resources. If this is the case, you should note this in this section and include this information on a separate sheet and attach it to the Course Record.

**3. Grading Method:** Parents should explain briefly how the grade given was determined. Was it on percentage of correct answers? Points for completed projects with so many required? Or was it subjective opinion of the parent? This is also the place to explain the number of hours which were required to earn the credit or portion of credit awarded. See Section IV, Planning Individual Courses, for more information on establishing evaluation criteria.

**4. Projects & Activities I participated in for this course:** You should list all projects (reports, field trips and special activities related to the subject in which you participated) even the ones you feel were not successful or ef-

fective. Save all papers or projects you completed in course envelopes. You may choose to save only the major projects, papers and tests. But be sure to save a fair representation of your work.

**5. What I gained from this course:** This is your place to describe what, if anything, you gained from this course. If it was review, say so. The main purpose of this section is to help you to recognize your own academic growth and to see the value in the work you are doing, so it's important to be candid in this section. Reviewing this section can be helpful when you are determining areas of interest and areas where you need additional help.

**6. Teacher Comments on Student's Progress:** This area is designed to allow parents/teachers to recognize your are academic as well as social and emotional growth as indicated by the work in this course. What important skills did you acquire? Is there a positive change in attitudes toward the subject or work in general being exhibited?

## Transcript/Report Card

This form serves as a report card and a permanent "official" transcript for home schooled students. The form provides a complete running list of courses completed for each year and has a space for a cumulative grade point. You will find this form helpful when you enroll in other programs, college or vocational school.

The term "Subject" in this instance refers to the area for which you are claiming credit. Some courses can be applied to more than one credit requirement. For example, Anatomy and Physiology can be a Health or a Biology credit. You need to declare which you are claiming it as, since you can not claim the same course twice. The "Course Description" area is for the specific name of the course. In the example above, you would insert Anatomy and Physiology.

The section marked "Ref #" refers to the Course Record number described above. This "Reference" will make it easy for you, or anyone evaluating your transcript, to compare it to the Course Record or to locate the envelope of sample work.

**Transcript/Report Card**

Name: _____  Expected Graduation: _____

Address: _____

Parent/Legal Guardian: _____  Birthdate: _____

Gender: _____  Notes: _____

| Date Completed | Subject | Course Description | Ref # | Attempted Credits | Credits Earned | Grade |
|---|---|---|---|---|---|---|
| | | | | | | |
| | | | | | | |
| | | | | | | |
| | | | | | | |
| | | | | | | |
| | | | | | | |
| | | | | | | |
| | | | | | | |
| | | | | | | |
| | | | | | | |
| | | | | | | |
| | | | | | | |
| | | | | | | |
| | | | | | | |
| | | | | | | |
| | | | | | | |
| | | End of Year Summary | | | | |
| | | To Date Summary | | | | |

© 1995 Castlemoyle Books

The "grade" section of the form should be recorded as a decimal number, with 4.0 equaling an A, 3.5 a B+, 3.0 a B, 2.5 a C+, 2.0 a C, 1.5 a D+, 1.0 a D, and 0.0 as a F. These are the most common decimal values used throughout the United States.

These forms should be photocopied for your permanent records at the end of each year and filed with your other academic records and important papers in a moisture and fire resistant box.

## Reading Record

The Reading Record is for your own information. It is basically a mini book report to remind you of what you have read. If your school or parents require you to read a certain number of "pleasure" books a year this is a great place to record them. If they do not, you may find it interesting to see just how many books you really do read and a record is the only way you will find out this information.

If you choose (or your parents require you) to keep a reading record, make sure you include this in the material you show to college admissions officers. It can make a difference. Some colleges are very interested in students who demonstrate that they are "well read."

A number of sources are available for suggestions of books to read. Among them are *The Dictionary of Cultural Literacy* by E. D. Hirsch, Jr. and *How to Read a Book* and *A Guidebook to Learning*, as well as a number of other books, by Mortimer J. Adler.

## Experience Record

This helpful form is designed to keep a record of projects and activities that are generally considered extra-curricular. Extra-curricular activities are an important consideration to many college admissions officers and future employers. The Experience Record is designed to help you keep a record of all the details of such activities and you will find them helpful when you complete college applications and job applications.

You should include job descriptions, descriptions of volunteer duties or basic descriptions of skills involved. Make sure that you include all volunteer work, paid employment, club/organization offices and involvement, special events, participation in academic competitions, and athletic (position on team, number of games and team performance) and hobby participation.

You should also keep a record of companies and people you have visited as you investigate career options, field trip type activities (including family vacations), and church and civic involvement. Participation in foreign exchange programs as an exchange student or a host family should also be included on an Experience Record.

If you have participated in a unique project for course work you may wish to duplicate the information about it in your Experience Record. What is more, the Experience Record can be a great aid to students who use the "unschooling" or "natural learning" approach to their home schooling. By keeping a record of activities as you do them you can later organize them into portfolios of course work.

One student kept an Experience Record on all his car maintenance and repairs during the year. He used the Chilton Manual for his car

**Reading record**

List books as you read them. You should list books read for pleasure as well as those read for your course work and projects.

Book title: _____
Author: _____
Publisher: _____ Copyright: _____ ISBN: _____
Describe briefly: _____
_____
_____
_____

Book title: _____
Author: _____
Publisher: _____ Copyright: _____ ISBN: _____
Describe briefly: _____
_____
_____
_____

Book title: _____
Author: _____
Publisher: _____ Copyright: _____ ISBN: _____
Describe briefly: _____
_____
_____
_____

© 1995 Cartesnople Books

and an automotive textbook to help him make the repairs and learn about the maintenance required. Near the end of the year he compared the work he had done on his car to the automotive textbook's chapters to determine which areas about which he still needed to learn. When he came up with the list of the things he still needed to master, he volunteered his services to family members and friends.

The next year, as a service project, he offered his mechanic services through the local senior center. For an entire year he made himself available every Thursday at the center. He did routine maintenance and repairs for over 50 seniors (mostly widows) during the school year. This work, besides being excellent course work, was personally rewarding to the young man.

He used his Experience Records later to get a job at an automotive dealership as a mechanic. The dealership sent him to various classes, sponsored by the manufacturer, allowing him to become a Certified Mechanic. Had he not kept a record of the types of repairs and maintenance he completed, as well as the letters of thanks from the people he

helped, he may not have been able to persuade the dealership to hire him in the first place.

It is a good idea to file these pages (in an envelope of their own) on a regular basis, say every term. More frequent filling would become cumbersome, whereas less frequent filling may lead to excessive numbers of pages in your planner and wear and tear on your records. You can refer to them as needed to complete applications or create resumes. You may find the Experience Summary Form (See Appendix E) helpful to create a summary for your binder.

# Creating Records for Previous Courses

If you are already in high school you may have already started or completed courses before beginning this course. Each of these courses must be documented as well. It may be a little more complicated working backward, but it will be well worth doing now, rather than waiting.

Begin by creating a Course Record Sheet for each course which you have completed. You probably already listed these courses on your Tentative High School Plan Sheet. If you are using a standard textbook approach, it will be fairly easy for you to complete a Course Record Sheet for each course you listed. If not, you may have a little more challenging task before you, but persevere.

Collect as many samples as possible of the work you completed for each course into course envelopes. Take pictures of larger projects and include them if at all possible. You should also go back and create an Experience Record for any activity that is not easily documented by sample work. Depending on how good your records are and the type of work you have completed you may need to simply declare you have taken and passed the course rather than have a set "grade." It may be helpful for you to review previous sections on course planning and use this information to help you determine credits and grades.

The next step, for all students, is to com-

---

**Experience Record**

Name: _____

Activity: _____

Date Begun: _____ Date Ended: _____

Where: _____

  Supervisor: _____

  Address: _____

  City, State, Zipcode: _____

  Phone Number: (____)_____

Description of Activity: _____

_____

_____

_____

_____

_____

_____

_____

_____

_____

_____

_____

_____

_____

© 1995 Castlemoyle Books

plete an Experience Record for any activity you have participated in since you started "high school" that has not been covered by course records. It's a good idea to group these by type of activity. This will help you recognize interest patterns and may even help you discover an area in which you have done significant "course work" and for which you may claim credit.

You should also complete Reading Record entries for as many of the books you have read

as possible. Again, you may find a pattern or see significant "course" material emerging. Combining this Reading Record with Project Documentation and Experience Records may result in a number of credits.

The final step, would be to summarize each year's efforts on to one Transcript/Report Card. When you have completed this documentation of past efforts you should be well prepared to maintain your records until graduation.

# Do You Really Need A High School Diploma?

When you have successfully completed and documented all of your high school courses (which were determined necessary in Section II), you will have completed your high school education. You will have an "Official Transcript" and a Portfolio of the work you completed during your high school years. You may be wondering if achieving these things means you have earned your Diploma and whether it means you have now graduated from high school. The answer to this question may depend on many factors, including where you live and your post high school goals and plans.

The majority of home schooled teens, who have met the suggested college bound requirement and documented them in terms that future employers and colleges can understand, have had no difficulty simply stating that they have graduated. As stated earlier, most colleges put more weight on the admissions scores and application information and most employers will not ask for an actual copy of a diploma. They generally only ask when and where you have graduated. Actually most colleges only ask the same. After all, a high school diploma is simply a document attesting to the fact that you have completed the required course of study with reasonable success. And graduating for the most part means you have been through a graduation ceremony at which you were presented the diploma you earned.

It's a simple matter to plan a graduation ceremony at home for your family and friends. Many families make it a joint effort by working with their local support group or their church community. Many state home school support

groups offer "graduation ceremonies" at which your parents can formally award you your diploma. The important thing is that it is an "Event" worthy of the milestone it represents.

For most students the diploma issued will be one issued from their "home school." Other families may choose to have a diploma issued from an accredited school. If this is your plan you need to check with the institution well before the end of your Junior year. Most schools will require you to complete at least one year's credits through them (this is true even of most public schools). This is generally required because

*Keeping a record of hands-on experiences and service projects can help you document course work.*

the school is attesting to your qualification and most schools feel it takes at least a year to verify the type and quality of work of which you are capable. In addition to the "seat" hours, the school may have specific graduation requirements that you need to be aware of as early in your high school years as possible.

Other families choose to back up their home school diploma with a G.E.D. Test. This is common with students who plan to enter the military. It is important to emphasize, however, that the G.E.D. is no substitute for meeting the normal high school requirements. The G.E.D. also may not meet your needs. Many, especially employers, see the G.E.D. as the diploma of the drop-out and it may be a negative. While this attitude is changing, use caution with this option.

Another option, especially if you are over 18, is to simply enroll in community college or vocational school courses. Community colleges and Vocational schools do not usually require a student over 18 to have a diploma. Once you have successfully completed a year or two at these schools it is fairly easy to transfer to a four year school. Actually, for college bound students, the two year transfer program is not

a bad idea anyway. Generally community colleges are smaller and less expensive per credit. You should check with the University you plan to attend to determine which and how many credits they will accept as transfer credits.

Whether you opt for the home school diploma, prefer to have your portfolio evaluated by an accredited institution to have a diploma issued, simply begin attending college, or take the G.E.D. test you will need to be sure that you have reached at least the minimum level of academic accomplishment expected of institutional school students. The purpose of this course up to this point has been to help you meet these expectations. You may need to review several aspects of this program each year to make sure you stay on track. It is also important that you check your Annual Checklists, which are found on the back of each year's Academic Year Planning Sheet, to make sure you are staying on track.

Contact your state home school association or Department of Instructions for information about requirements for graduation and organizations offering diplomas. See the list in Appendix D for how to contact your state association of Department of Instruction.

*For most students, the diploma issued will be from their "home school."*

# Exercises

## Exercise XX:

Set up a filing system for your course work. If you have already taken high school courses, organize samples of the work (if you can) and with your parents create Course Records for them. Enter your Courses on your Transcript/ Report Cards.

## Exercise XXI:

Create an Experience Record for as many activities as you can remember (at least two). Label the Fourth Tab Section of your planner-binder "Experience Records." Store all completed forms here until the end of the term when they can be transferred to a "Course Envelope"

of their own. Keep a Summary of Experiences in the front of this section.

## Exercise XXII:

A) Think of some of the books you have read and really enjoyed since beginning high school and make a Reading Record for each of those books. Store completed Reading Records behind the fifth tabbed section of your planner/ binder. You should Label this section Reading Record.

B) Set a goal for yourself to read a good book every month.

# Graduation Resources

The Home School Legal Defense Association offers a generic diploma. The parent fills out and signs it. You may obtain it for about $15 by writing to Home School Legal Defense Association at P.O. Box 159, Paionian Springs, VA 22129.

Home School Associates of New England offers a diploma issued by the "North Atlantic Regional School." This diploma is awarded by them after they have evaluated your portfolio. The cost is $60. For more information you may write them at 116 3rd Ave., Auburn, ME 04210.

Josten's offers a generic diploma for about $10. This is a certificate that the parent fills out and signs. Josten's also offers a complete line of graduation caps and gowns, announcements and class rings. Call 1-800-323-9343 for more information.

The Guide to PA (Pennsylvania) Homeschoolers Diploma, by Howard and Susan Richman provides information for Pennsylvania Home schoolers on receiving a high school diploma (only available to Pennsylvania students). The 32 page guide is available for $5 by writing them.

Texas Tech University offers Advanced Placement and credit by exam (as well as High school diplomas) materials and information to home schoolers. You may contact them at Box 42191, Lubbock, TX 79409 or by calling 1-800-MY COURS.

Oral Roberts University Home Education Center offers a program which allow home schoolers to earn a high school diploma while simultaneously earning college credits. You may contact them at P.O. Box 701476, Tulsa, OK 74170-1476. (918) 495-6621.

The University of Missouri Center for Independent Study has a number of programs of interest to home schooled high schoolers. In addition to correspondence school via video and computers. Tutoring services are offered via E-mail. You may contact them at University Extension, University of Missouri, 136 Clark Hall, Columbia, MO. 65211 or 1- 800-609-3727.

# SECTION 8

## Making Plans For After High School

*Most people require some sort of post high school education to prepare for the career of their choice. In Section 2 you considered your possible career goals and post high school education needs to help you determine what you needed to take in high school to progress toward your goals. In this section we return to explore your post high school education options and learn more about making decisions in this area.*

# A World of Opportunity and Options
# Are Available to Home School Graduates

When you complete your high school education you will be at the threshold of a whole new world of options and decisions. And now is not too soon to begin thinking about these options. Some students will find direct entry into the job-market or starting a business of their own the best choice. Many young ladies will decide to prepare for their role as wives and mothers. For most students, however, the next step will be some form of higher or post high school education or a combination of the above.

Post high school education comes in all shapes and sizes, just like the people who pursue it. Your changes range from very academic programs such as medical or engineering schools to very hands-on approaches such as culinary arts schools. Which type of program is best for you will be determined by your person-ality, academic or other strengths, and your career objectives. Let's take a look at the various options you may consider.

## Direct Entry into the
## Job-Market is One Option

For some students, especially those who still have not determined their career goals at the end of their high school years, the best option is direct entry into the job market. Many students who are choosing this option enter the job-market before they graduate from high school, usually as a part-time employee. Others enter or continue working for the family business.

There are many jobs that do not need higher education or offer training on the job. It used to be thought that the only jobs for people who have not gone on to college were lower paying jobs. That is not necessarily the case any longer. Unions have greatly raised the wages of workers. There are a number of excellent opportunities for employment with the government, (i.e. letter carrier), large corporations, and local chain store, as well as small business.

Some home schooled teens have started their own businesses, either during their high school years or upon completion. If you are interested in starting your own business you may find that you can research your prospects as part of your education. A number of home schoolers have designed courses that reflect their interest in entrepreneurship. For instance you may be able to earn composition credits for writing a business plan. Or may be you need "business math" or accounting to succeed in business. You should discuss with your parents how you can combine your high school courses with your interest in starting a business.

*Apprenticeships, vocational schools, and direct entry into the job market offer college alternatives.*

# Vocational Educational Opportunities After High School

Most communities have community colleges or vocational-technical schools which offer vocational-occupational programs. These programs vary in length from a few weeks to two years and provide courses in agriculture education, marketing, and business education, health occupations, home economics education, and office occupations, technical education, and trade and industrial education. In addition, there are private trade and technical schools which provide job training in limited areas, such as the Truck Driving Institute.

Most Vocational or Trade schools do not require a "high school diploma" and many accept students as young as 16 years of age. Of course, specific courses may have special course requirements. Upon completion of a vocational program most students have sufficient knowledge for an entry level position in the field. Usually you will receive a "Certificate of Training" which will let potential employers know you are ready for the job. These courses of study tend to be more hands-on in nature and less "theory" driven.

## Apprenticeships Offer Hands-On Opportunities

Apprenticeships offer a unique opportunity to "Earn as You Learn." An apprenticeship is a training program based upon a written agreement between the worker (apprentice) and the employer in which the worker learns a skilled trade or craft on the job. Most apprenticeship programs require more than one year of on-the-job training under the supervision of an experienced worker plus additional course work. Sometimes this course work is completed through a vocational or community college by special arrangement.

Application for apprenticeship may be made to an employer (e.g. Boeing), labor union (e.g. Electrician's Union), a joint apprenticeship and training committee, or the local state employment service office. You may also find more information regarding apprenticeships in the phone book under *apprenticeship council*.

## Opportunities in the Military

A high school graduate (or someone with a G.E.D) who enlists in the Air Force, Army, Coast Guard, Navy, or Marine Corps will have the opportunity to select a military occupation specialty. The military services invest great amounts of money in formal and on-the-job training in each of hundreds of occupational specialities.

In a four-year enlistment, for example, a person can receive the equivalent of a junior college education in occupational areas such as business management and administration, communications (electronic), technology, aircraft maintenance, photography, automotive mechanics, medical technology, transportation and traffic management, computer technology and operations, police science, fire protection technology, nursing, restaurant management, purchasing, accounting, and physical therapy assistant.

In some occupational areas, such as engineering and nursing, the military services will

*The military offers many educational opportunities.*

send a person through four or more years of college, if that person will agree to an extended period of enlistment. The Army and Navy have programs to aid a person as a civilian through nursing training (four-year college program), if the person will serve an extended enlistment as an officer. These examples only hint at the opportunities for learning while earning in the armed forces. Students may get specific information by talking to the local recruiting officers of each service.

# College Bound Students Have Options Too

There are two distinctive types of college programs — community colleges and four-year colleges. Community colleges (in some parts of the country they are still called Junior Colleges) generally offer two-year degrees or "certificates of training." A two year degree is also referred to as an Associate Degree. It generally qualifies individuals to work with another more experienced individual in their chosen field. For Example a person with an Associate Degree in Civil Engineering will work under an experienced civil engineer. Often people use an associative degree as a stepping-stone to college or their career.

Community colleges generally cost approximately half of what a university does per year. Therefore, students will often try to obtain as many "transferable" credits as possible at the community college before going on to a four year college. As a home schooler you have two other very good reasons to begin at a community college. First, a community college is generally smaller and makes a good transition from "home" to school. Second, attending a community college first usually side-steps the whole diploma issue. If you have succeeded in courses on the community college level, the four year college admissions counselor is easily convinced that you are prepared to attend his school.

A four-year college usually offers a Bachelor's Degree upon completion of the course of study. A Bachelor's Degree, allows you to begin working in the chosen field or to take the "certification" examination for the field. For instance, most classroom teachers are required to have a Bachelor's Degree before they can take the certification exam. This is also true of accountants and some types of engineers. Other occupations such as business managers, newspaper reporters, and public relations directors can enter directly into their field.

Most often students will attend a four-year college at a university. A university is a school which offers a number of four-year colleges (also called schools) on a single campus. For example, the University of Washington is composed of a Medical School, Journalism School, Engineering School, and so on. As opposed to universities, colleges are generally focused on a limited areas of study, for example Multnomah Bible college. In the case of the "Bible College" the focus is on theology or religion. A university also generally offers advanced programs, such as Masters and Doctorate (Ph.D.) degrees.

Acceptance to a state-supported community college is usually dependent only on possession of a high school diploma (see: "Do You Really Need a Diploma?" in Section VII for more information on this issue) and sufficiently early application. However, some states require students to pass an entrance test to take college level courses. However, acceptance at a community college does not insure that credits earned there necessarily will be accepted at a four-year institution. You should discuss, with the admissions director of colleges to which you are considering transferring, which and under what circumstances credits are transferable.

Applications to two and four-year colleges in your own state are usually available from the counseling office of your local high school. However, you may also call or write to the colleges to receive an application. You will almost always have to write to out of state schools.

## Getting Into A University

Acceptance at a four-year college in or out of the state can be very competitive. Most admissions officers are interested in the qualitative nature of achievements (your portfolio and test scores) as well as in supportive comments written on your behalf by former teachers, pastors or priests, family friends, past employers and so on. These are referred to as "letters of recommendation."

You should begin requesting letters of recommendation as soon as possible. If you take any formal classes (at a school or through private lessons), ask the teacher for a letter of recommendation upon completion, even if you will not be applying to college for three more years. It will be much harder to locate the teacher in three years and harder for the teacher to write it as well as they may have forgotten you. Submitting letters, collected over a period of time, also shows the consistency of your personality. This may make you a more desirable candidate than the student who col-lected his letters during the two week period just before application.

Because housing frequently is a problem, you should apply as soon as possible for on-campus housing if you will be living away from home. Generally housing information should be requested at the same time an admissions application is submitted.

Most schools charge an application fee ranging from $15 to $75. You should plan for this expense when saving for college. (Waivers of these fees may be granted in special cases. An admissions director can give you information on this.) Most four-year colleges request that applications be sent to their admissions office beginning December 1. However, students applying to the service academies or for ROTC scholarships must do so in the spring of their Junior year or in the summer prior to their senior year. It is wise to check each individual college deadline.

## A Correspondence Program May Allow You To Home School In College

Correspondence programs, which allow you to acquire your post high school education through home schooling, are available for many of the types of programs already discussed in this section. There are college courses available by mail or through television, video, and/or computer courses. Some programs are offered strictly through the mail. You will also find many programs for vocational training as well. For more information you should contact the American Association of Correspondence Schools.

*You may be able to continue home schooling during college.*

# Things to Consider in Choosing a College

Your college education will be a big investment in time, talent and money by both you and your parents. Good solid planning and careful, prayerful consideration are required if this investment is to be worthwhile. The following areas are those which you should consider.

**1. God's Will** -- As you read college literature, visit campuses, and so on you should take the time to pray for God's discernment in the area of choosing your college. The college or university you choose will often times be your home for the next four years. It is important that this be a place you feel comfortable and can grow in all areas of your life — not just academically.

**2. Religious affiliation** — Many colleges are run by religious organizations or have a specific Christian emphasis. Is this important to you? If the school is not a Christian college, do they have a dorm, fraternity, or other housing specifically for students of your faith? Is there an organization or meeting house for Christian students or students of your denomination? How far from campus or your housing will you have to travel to find a suitable church community. Being able to establish relationships with like-minded students will greatly ease your adjustment to college life.

**3. Excellence of subject area of interest** — Which schools have the best reputation for the area of study you have chosen? You may find a large selection of books, such as *Comparative Guide to American Colleges* by Cass and Birnbaum, at the public library a helpful resource in this area.

**4. Size** — Some young people find that they do better at smaller colleges (at least at the beginning) than at a large college or university. Class size can also be a major factor for a student used to a more one-on-one program. These considerations make it very important that you find out both the physical size and population of a college, as well as the average class size of the types of courses you will be taking.

**5. Location** — Think about what kind of geographic area might best suit you. For example, why consider a place with lots of snow if you dislike this kind of climate? If you have always lived in the country how will you react to life in a big city and vice versa? The cost of travel to and from home is also an important factor. Speaking of distance from home, you should consider how you and your family will deal with being apart from one-another for long periods.

**6. College campus** — Anyone planning to spend four years at a college should visit the campus. While, similar in consideration to location, this element focuses on some of the more specific aspects of the college such as its layout and the availability of housing. If you would like to travel to and from classes on your bike a college built on a hill side might make this impossible. Such a site would also have ramification for students with handicaps.

**7. Cost** — In-state public colleges and universities generally cost less than out of state schools and private colleges and universities. This is because most public colleges are at least partially tax supported. They generally charge less for residents (who presumably have paid taxes to support the school.) Costs vary, however, so do not assume that because a school is out of state it will cost more. Check first.

**8. Financial aid** — A financial aid package can include a scholarship, grant, loan, part-time employment, and work-study programs. Read Section IX (Paying for College) for more details.

**9. Admissions criteria** — Can you get in? What are the entrance requirements? What kind of ACT-SAT scores will be required to be considered? At some colleges, competition is high and space is limited, but many colleges have an open admission policy and will admit anyone.

**10. Foreign Language** — Many colleges require a foreign language for admission; you should be aware of this possibility. You should check the catalog of the college being considered for its requirements, and be aware of language requirements when planning your high school course of study. Sometimes students can obtain their foreign language credits at the community college.

**11. Activities other than academic** — Is a foreign-exchange program offered? Are there foreign language houses on campus? Is there a drama club or student theater? An orchestra? Band? Choir? Athletics?

**12. ROTC programs** — Reserve Officer Training Programs can provide considerable financial aid. If this is a program you want to participate in you will need to make sure the college offers it.

**13. Tests** — College tests may be taken more than once. Be certain you are taking the appropriate admissions test for any school which you are considering.

# Additional Tips Regarding College Selection

Here are a few additional helpful hints on how you may obtain more information about a college you are considering.

☑    Talk with the college representatives when they visit local schools. Write to the college and ask when and at which schools they will be visiting.

☑    Attend college information and financial aid programs.

☑    Talk with the public high school counselor. Ask questions. Most states prohibit the schools from denying services to home schoolers. So, if you think the information available will be useful, you should take advantage of it.

☑    Talk with students or parents who are familiar with the college that you are considering. Often the school will give you names and addresses of local alumni. You can also ask family friends and relatives if they know anyone who has attended the school. It is not necessary that they have graduated from that school. Often the reason the person dropped out of the school can be just as valuable to know.

# Exercises

## Exercise XXIII

Interview at least five adults to find out how and where they completed their post high school education.

## Exercise XXIV

If you plan to attend some form of post high school education, start investigating your options and start a dialog with the schools you may be considering.

# SECTION 9

# Paying For Post High School Education

*The end of your eighth grade year is not too early to begin thinking about how you plan to pay for your college or vocational education. In this section you will learn about some of the common ways young people save for and pay for their higher education. You will also make some of your own plans to prepare financially for college or other higher education.*

# Academic Competitions and Contests

Many students get a jump on the high costs of college by beginning to enter academic competitions and other contests beginning in sixth grade, and even younger. Academic competitions and contests generally require that you submit an essay, art project, or participate in some other way in contests. Many of these competitions provide small to medium monetary prizes or savings bonds for college tuition. The volume and variety of these programs are too numerous to mention here so instead I will direct you to a number of excellent resources for scholarship information. You will find these listed under College Planning Resources in Appendix C. Do not wait until the end of your Junior or Senior year to check out these books.

With a little or lot (depending on the individual) of effort you can build quite a nest egg for your college education. One creative individual even searched for essay and project scholarships based on related themes each year. This allowed him to do one massive research project and then prepare the information in a number of formats to meet the specific requirements of the different competitions. This saved enormous work for the student and won him several prizes of U.S. Savings Bonds for college. You will also find that many of the topics of academic competitions are related to reports you have to do for your course work anyway. What is more, many home school parents are willing to give their children English credits or credits in related subjects for work they have done preparing for academic competitions.

The best book for younger students and those wishing to consolidate research is the book *Contests for Students* by Mary Ellen Snodgrass. This is one book that you should consider owning, the others listed in the Appendix C can be borrowed from your local library.

Whenever you participate in one of these competitions, make sure you record your efforts on your Experience Record Forms and include them on your college or employment application resumes. Both colleges and employers take a positive interest in young people who are involved and persistent. They understand the learning and discipline it takes to participate in such events. This type of record will set you apart from the other hundreds of students applying for a job or entrance to a school. With this point in mind, you can see entering academic competitions (in addition to being interesting) can be a positive for you even if you do not win a cash or scholarship prize.

*Competitions may allow you to get a jump-start on your college funding.*

# Scholarships Can Make College a Reality

Thousands of scholarships are awarded each year to deserving young people. Generally scholarships are based on either some kind of achievement or on need. Most of what are considered traditional scholarships should be applied for near the end of your Junior year or during your Senior year of high school. Basically, there are five kinds of scholarships available:

**1. Academic:** This is generally based on a student's cumulative grade-point average (GPA) for grades 9-12, but often college entrance exam scores can be combined with GPA or used alone to determine scholarship eligibility. Many academic scholarships are offered by colleges, especially private colleges, but many other sources are available. To qualify for the National Merit Scholarship you must take the PSAT during your Junior year of high school. See Appendix B Testing Information and Summaries for details.

**2. Talent:** Art, music, drama, and the like are considered in this category. An audition, performance competition, or portfolio is usually required from the student. The individual department of the college should be contacted by the student about talent scholarships.

**3. Athletic:** A high school or other team coach, the college coach, and the counselor generally confer about students who are candidates for athletic scholarships.

**4. Miscellaneous:** Memorial scholarships, trust funds, community organizations, honorary (no financial aid), professional organizations, employers, unions, and such offer many grant-type scholarships. Most high schools and colleges publish an annual list of these scholarships: check with the colleges you are considering. The competition for many of these scholarships is not as tough as you would think. In fact, many of them are restricted to very specific types of individuals (e.g. employee's children) and go un-awarded each year.

A good resource for finding these scholarships is the *College Planning Network's Pacific*

*Northwest Scholarship Options Guide.* Make sure that you are looking at the current volume, as they change annually. Also, you should check with your parents' (and often grandparents') employers, union, or any other organization (Elks, Eagles, etc.) to which they may belong to see if you are eligible for any of these scholarships.

**5. Financial Need:** Many organizations offer scholarships to students based mainly on financial needs. A good share of the scholarships in this category are offered to minorities, young people from target or disadvantaged areas, and to young women wishing to study in non-traditional (for women) jobs. If you have a genuine financial need, and you put in your homework, you are sure to find a program for which you qualify.

While researching scholarships and making all of the applications is tedious, demanding work it will pay off. Having a scholarship can actually help you get into the college of your choice, if you know about it early enough in your senior year. Therefore, make sure any college you are considering knows about the Scholar-

### Scholarships Earned

(Store Documents in Safe Deposit Box or Metal File Cabinet)

| Date | Title | Purpose | Value |
|------|-------|---------|-------|
|      |       |         |       |
|      |       |         |       |
|      |       |         |       |
|      |       |         |       |
|      |       |         |       |
|      |       |         |       |
|      |       |         |       |
|      |       |         |       |
|      |       |         |       |
|      |       |         |       |
|      |       |         |       |
|      |       |         |       |
|      |       |         |       |
|      |       |         |       |
|      |       |         |       |
|      |       |         |       |
|      |       |         |       |

© 1995 Castlemyle Books                    Bonds 3/94

ship and Competition awards you have received. The Scholarship Chart (see Appendix E) can be used to help you keep a record of these awards. They should be filed in the Financial Section (sixth tabbed divider) of your Planner/binder.

## Financial Aid Available

Most money for meeting college costs is provided through financial aid programs. To apply for this money, fill out a Financial Aid Form (FAF) or Family Financial Statement (FFS). These forms are available in the counseling office or career center of your local high school or from the colleges you have selected to attend. Some colleges have their own supplemental forms as well and you should request them when you request your admissions applications kit.

Financial aid information is listed in most college catalogs and in many other college books, such as *Barron's Guide to the Two-Year*

*Colleges, Barron's Profiles of American Colleges, Lovejoy's College Guide* and *College Blue Book.*

The FAF or FFS must be submitted after January 1 of your Senior year (or the year before you plan to begin college). Begin to fill out the FAF and/or FFS forms as soon as you have the information on you and your parents' last year's income. The deadline for receiving the completed financial aid form varies from college to college, but, generally, March 1 is a common deadline (it is preferable to mail forms by February 1 to allow processing time.

Parents are strongly urged to complete the FAF or FFS form because so many financial aid programs, including state and federal, require the FAF or FFS. Also, keep in mind that need is not determined solely on income, but on a combination of many variables (such as other children in college), as well as on the cost of the college. Another source of aid may be low-interest loans from banks and credit unions.

## Begin Your Own Savings As Soon As Possible

*Starting your own business is a common source of income for home school teens.*

Young people considering any type of higher education should immediately open a savings account for that purpose. This, in these times of high unemployment and tougher regulations for employers, may not be as easy as it once was but it is possible. Many home school teens find it easier to obtain employment because of their flexible hours. Others make school projects out of running their own small business.

There are many excellent books on starting and running your own business, even some which are written just for teens. If self-employment sounds interesting to you, one excellent resource is *Capitalism For Kids. The Teen-Age Liberation Handbook* is full of helpful information as well. I suggest after you have read a few of the teen books you check out those written for adult entrepreneurs.

Whether you get a job or create a job for yourself, you need to begin a savings plan. The Income and Expense Record forms (see Appendix E) offer you a simple form to record your income and expenses, as well as your savings.

Your parents will surely be glad to help you work out a budget and savings plan. Consult them. You and your parents also might find the

"Monthly Money" program an excellent resource for your budgeting needs. Monthly Money is listed in Appendix C.

# Ways You Can Reduce The Cost of College

Another way to help finance your college education is by reducing the cost. There are a number of programs that you can take advantage of during your high school and college years to reduce the cost of your college education, including Advanced Placement Exams, challenge examinations and early entry programs.

## You can't lose with AP  Tests

Taking the Advanced Placement (AP) courses and exams is a Win-Win situation. AP Exams are given each May to high school students around the country in subjects ranging from Art to Latin. These exams are designed to determine if you have acquired at least a first quarter college level of proficiency in the subject area. The test scores range from 1 to 5 points. If your score is three or above you do not have to take the subject as a prerequisite to advanced courses in the subject and you receive 5 college credits for your efforts. If you score two points or below you do not have to take prerequisites to take the advanced courses, but you do not receive college credit. Either way, you also receive high school credits for the study and work you did to prepare for the exam.

There is no limit on the number of subjects you can test for, however some colleges will only accept so many for college credits. Even if you are not receiving college credit, the exams are well worth it because you will raise your scores on other entrance exams and also look a more promising student to college admission officers. The tests usually cost about $35 per subject.

You do not need to be enrolled in a specific class to sit for the exams, but you should get the materials which will outline what you need to study to prepare for the exams. In studying for any course for which you intend to take an

Advanced Placement Test you should use a college textbook not the typical high school text. For more information on Advanced Placement examinations you should speak to the counselor at your local high school or write to The College Board at Box 886, New York, New York 10101-0886. As you can see, Advanced Placement programs allow you to begin your college education as a home schooled high school student.

## Double-up with Early Entry

Early entry programs are another interesting option. Many states offer such programs to allow "able students" to enter community college. Often it is free to such students. Usually the student can earn both college and high school credit. Check with your local community college for the existence and rules governing such programs in you area. Below is a description of how the program operates in Washington State.

The early entry program for Washington State students is called Project Running Start. This program is designed to let "talented" students begin taking college courses during high school. Many home schoolers have done extremely well on the entrance examination (see Appendix B, ASSET test). Sponsored by the State Department of Instruction, you may be able to complete much of your first two years of college on this program. You must be 16 years of age and/or reached Junior status (beginning of Junior year) to take advantage of the program. You can enter the program at anytime you meet or exceed these two requirements and have passed the entrance exam (You may take the entrance exam more than once). Through this program you may only earn the number of credits you require to graduate from high school. (Five college credits equal three-fourths to one high school credit.) While the courses are free, you must purchase your own books and supplies. Some colleges require you to enroll through your local public high school.

When you participate in an early entry program, you attend classes at the community college as a regular college student. Therefore, you will be treated as a college student who takes responsibility for your own work and maturity. Most students participating only attend the college part time and work on their other course at their regular school (or home school). Such programs offer home schooled students an excellent opportunity to earn advanced mathematics and foreign language credits, that are sometimes hard to study on your own. For more information about the program you should contact your local community college or local high school.

## Earn Credit by Challenging the Course

Another way you can reduce college costs is by taking College Level Examination Program (CLEP) tests and other similar tests. CLEP tests can be taken to show proficiency in a subject as well as to receive an exemption for a prerequisite class. Since these tests are "college level" they can also be used to show that you are prepared for college level courses. Unlike AP tests, you can take CLEP tests at many times of the year.

Some colleges also offer "credit by examination" credits. These programs require you to take an examination to prove you "know" the subject. The exams are generally more difficult than the classes' final exam. The cost of such tests vary - some cost the same as if you took the course. Even at the full tuition rate the testing may save you money, if you can study for the course/exam off campus.

Like transferring from community college, many colleges have a limit on the number of credits which can be earned through testing programs. College's also often have policies on the total number of credits earned "off campus" (from any combination of transfer and testing) as well. Generally the purpose is similar to the "seat hour" conditions at high schools. Be sure you check with the admissions advisor of any college you plan to attend regarding these policies. These policies should be a factor in your comparison of college costs.

# Exercises

## Exercise XIX

Enter all your savings for college and scholarships earned to date on the Scholarship and Bond Summary. File these in the sixth section of your binder (Label it Financial). You should also include the 12 copies of the monthly Income and Expense forms you copied from the masters provided in Appendix E. Make sure you enter additional bonds, scholarships, etc. as you acquire them.

## Exercise XX

Appendix C provides a list of resources that will help you identify competitions you can enter. Obtain a copy of at least one of these books (from the library or bookstore) and examine them. Set a goal to enter at least one academic or scholarship competition each year, until you graduate.

## Exercise XXI

Discuss your college or vocational school ambitions with your parents. Together work out a financial plan and employment program that will allow you to earn and save money for your higher education. Set a goal of how much of your higher education you will pay for out of your own efforts and how much you hope to save towards it each year.

Use the forms provided in the Financial Section of your plan book to establish a budget for yourself. Make a date with yourself each month to go over your expenses and savings account. Your parents and the forms provided will help you establish good habits of financial stewardship. You may find several of the books in the Bibliography - Additional Suggested Reading List (Appendix C) helpful.

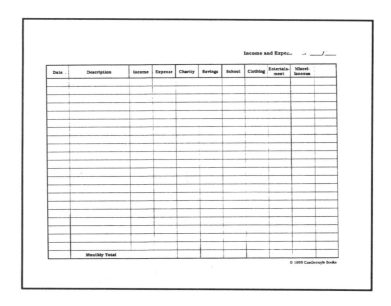

# AFTERWORD

Filling out all these different forms may seem like a lot of work and very time consuming. You can see, however, that each form has its own function quite apart from the others. What is more, each form builds on the others. Scheduling should take you less than 10 to 20 minutes a day at most. The more you practice using the Goal Setting, Organization, and Time Management tools in this program the faster you will be at it. A quick review will help put it in perspective.

You will be spending time at the beginning of each year (or at the end of the year you are finishing) mapping out what subjects you will be studying during the coming year. Then before each term, you will make detailed plans for each course, including Course Requirement Sheets and Project Planning Sheets for any and all major assignments due during the term. These forms and tools provide the skeleton or framework for your home schooling studies. As you complete assignments you will file samples of your work in your course envelopes.

Then you will spend 15 to 20 minutes at the beginning of each month going over your goals and schedule. You will spend an additional 10 to 15 minutes each Sunday evening or Monday morning going over your weekly schedule. Finally you will spend 5 to 10 minutes each evening or morning preparing for your next day.

If you have been faithfully completing all of the exercises as they have been assigned, you should be well on your way to using your time effectively and efficiently. As you continue toward your educational and career goals keep working on perfecting your time management and study skills. I know you will find it rewarding.

I pray God will continue to guide and Bless you on your journey through this life as you continue to prepare to join Him in the next.

Beverly L. Adams-Gordon

Author

# Appendix A

## Topics and Course Ideas For High School Students

## English Courses

Three English credits are required and may be satisfied by any combination of Literature, grammar, composition, spelling, vocabulary, and library-study skills. Most standard high-school English texts include a combination of grammar, composition, spelling, vocabulary, and library skills. Literature courses are usually contained in separate texts and usually include writing and vocabulary activities.

Speech
Drama
Composition
Debate
Children's Theater
Basic Grammar
Journalism
Newswriting
Practical Writing
Creative Writing
Research Process
Basic Reading
Spelling
Business English
Vocational English
Report Writing
Freshman English
Sophomore English
Junior English
Senior English
AP English

Poetry
Essay Composition
Precis' Writing
Letter Writing
Advertising
Business Letter Writing
Ballads
Beginning Novel Writing
Biography
Book Reviews
Library Skills
Reference Skills
Film
Expository Writing
Parliamentary Procedure
Allegory
Mythology: Greek
Mythology: Roman
Fiction
History of English
Lear, Limericks, & Literature

Propaganda Analysis
Study Skills
Analytical Thinking
Science Fiction Writing
Roots to English
Periodical Literature
American Literature
Theater Shakespeare
Intro. To Literature
New Testament Literature
English Literature
The Epic
Old Testament Literature
Script Writing
American Poets
World Literature
Western Literature
Great Books Programs
AP Literature
Contemporary American
Novels

## Health Education Courses

Lifestyle Choices
Health
Nutrition
Safety & First Aid
CPR Training

Child Development
Food Sanitation
Sex Education
Anatomy & Physiology
Community Health

Drug Education
Death & Dying
AIDS Education
Mental Health
Fitness & Weight Control

# Mathematics Courses

Two credits of Mathematics are required to graduate, however students who plan to enter a four year college should take four years. If you plan to enter a technical career you must take advanced or college prep mathematics (✍ marks suggested courses).

9th Grade Math
Computational Math
Senior Math
Applied Math
Consumer Mathematics
Intro to High School Math
Business Math
Accounting
Vocational Math
Algebra 1 ✍

Algebra 2 w/Trig. ✍
Geometry ✍
Pre-Calculus ✍
Math Analysis ✍
Calculus ✍
AP Calculus ✍
Banks and Banking
Budgeting
Computer
Logic

Computer Programming
Graphs and Tables
Math Analysis
Investment
Math for Science
How to Lie with Statistics
Measurement
Economics
Taxation
Personal Finance

# Science Courses

Two credits are required, at least one of which is a laboratory science. For a course to qualify for a laboratory science, the student should be involved with experimentation, investigations, observation and the study and practice of the skills used by scientists. Simply studying the textbook and taking the tests does not meet the laboratory science requirements.

General Science
Earth Science
Biology
Botany
Zoology
Astronomy
Ecology
Oceanography
Marine Biology

Chemistry
Physics
Physical Science
Anthropology
Creation Science
Space Travel
Microscopic Life
Invertebrate Life
Nuclear Science & Technology

Space, Time & Motion
Reproduction & Growth
Genetics
Health & Safety
Nuclear Physics
Pollution
Inventioneering
Disease & Disease Control

# Physical Education Courses

The two credit physical education/health requirement shall be met by course work in the areas of personal fitness development, leisure activities, health education/life skills management, and healthful living.

Tennis
Swimming
Aerobics
Ballet
Martial Arts
Hiking
Skiing
Archery
Marksmanship

Recreational Sports
Team Sports
Gymnastics
Jazzersize
Golf
Mountaineering
Snowshoeing
Bicycling
Sailing

Weight Training & Cond.
Jogging
Dance
Karate
Life Guard Training
Cross-Country Skiing
Volksmarching
Equestrian Competition
Track & Field

# Social Studies Courses

One credit is required in United States history and government which shall include study of the Constitution of the United States. No other course content may be substituted as an equivalency for this requirement. One-half credit is usually required in state history and government which shall include the study of the Constitution of the State. The state history and government course requirement may be fulfilled by students in grades seven or eight or both. Credits earned in grades seven or eight shall not be applied toward the minimum number of credits required for high school graduation. One credit is required in contemporary world history, geography, and problems. Courses in economics, sociology, civics, political science, international relations, or related courses with emphasis on current problems may be accepted as equivalencies.

| | | |
|---|---|---|
| World History | State History & Government | Cultures & Civilizations |
| World Social Studies | Peoples of the Pacific Rim | Contemporary Wld Problems |
| U.S. History | Twentieth Century Europe | Political Analysis |
| Political & Economic Systems | Justice | American Political Systems |
| AP American History | Bible History | AP European History |
| Global Geography | Native American Studies | Early World History |
| Intro. To Sociology | Intro. to Psychology | Current Events |
| Multicultural Studies | American Heroes | Western Civilization |
| The Crusades | Development of Democracy | Civics |
| History of Western Hemisphere | American Government | Church History |
| National History Day | Philosophy | Free Market Economics |

# Fine Arts Courses

Fine Arts classes include drama, art, and music. Classes may be practical or appreciative in nature at the student's or teacher's discretion.

## Music

| | | |
|---|---|---|
| Music Theory | Guitar | Instruments |
| Concert Band | Symphonic Band | String Band |
| Women's Choir | Men's Choir | Choir |
| Vocal Ensemble | Musical Production | Piano |
| Music History | Music Appreciation | The Opera |

## Art

| | | |
|---|---|---|
| General Art | General Crafts | Commercial Art |
| Drawing | Art Appreciation | Art History |
| Ceramics | Pottery | Silkscreening |
| Photography | Poster Design | Origami |
| Calligraphy | Jewelry & Metal Design | Weaving |
| Sculpting | Painting Oils | Painting Watercolor |
| Painting Acrylics | Native Arts & Crafts | Beading |

## Performing Arts

| | | |
|---|---|---|
| Dance | Ballet | Mime |
| Theater | Shakespeare | Interpretive Reading |

# Occupational Education

This includes, but is not limited to, homemaking, industrial arts, business and office occupations, trade and industrial education. Courses such as 'Time Management' are considered Occupational Education. Do not forget to give yourself credit for working through this book, if you are in grade nine or above.

Some students choose to earn this credit through work experience and by maintaining a journal of work experience. A Work Experience credit requires supervision by a teacher, being past your sixteenth birthday, legal employment (may be volunteer, if your work does not displace a paid employee), employer provided reports of student's work record. You must include at least four hundred five (405) hours or more of work experience related to your school program. (Work experience credits may be applied to elective requirements or to occupational education requirement. A student may not earn more than one work experience credit.)

| | | |
|---|---|---|
| Typing/Keyboarding | Note-Taking | Shorthand |
| Word Processing | Business Machines | Business Law |
| Business Principles | Intro. to Business | Economics |
| Time Management * | Accounting | Recordkeeping |
| Intro. to Computers | Marketing | Cooking |
| Marriage & Family Life | Fashion Design | Sewing |
| Interior Decorating | Drafting | Carpentry |
| Exploring Childhood | Consumer Skills | CAD Drafting |
| Culinary Arts | Medical Assistant | Diesel Mechanics |
| Home Furnishing | Woodworking | Automotive |
| Small Engine Repair | Computer Technology | Electronics |
| Metalworking | Cabinet Making | Retail Sales |
| Entrepreneurship | Work Experience | Visual Communication |
| Office Assistant | | |

# Foreign Language Education

| | | |
|---|---|---|
| French ** | Latin | Survey of Languages |
| Japanese | German | Spanish |
| Greek | Russian ** | Chinese ** |
| Norwegian | Swedish | Irish |
| Sign Language/Manual English | | |

# Miscellaneous Education

Courses that are selected to meet college admission requirements or to satisfy interests of the students. To satisfy minimum high school requirements, for most states, you need at least five and a half (5.5) elective credits. In addition to the following subjects, any credit beyond the minimum required for a subject area may be used as an elective credit.

| | | |
|---|---|---|
| Study Hall | Driver's Ed. | Teacher's Aide |
| Study Skills | Office Aide | Library Aide |
| Alternative Learning Experience | Religious Education | |

*The work you do to complete the exercises which go along with this book are equal to one-quarter credit in Occupational Education. Make sure you make a record of your work on your course record.

**These three languages, English, and Sign Language are the most commonly used languages of the world.

# Appendix B
## Testing Information and Summaries

### Achievement tests
In many states, all home schooled students between the ages of eight and eighteen, are required to take an annual achievement test administered by a qualified individual. The results of these tests can be used profitably to help you select appropriate courses (particularly in the areas of math and the language arts), identify weak areas, and help make career choices. You and your parents should request an interpretation of the test scores from the test administrator.

Public and private schools administer these tests at different intervals, usually 10th grade. If you are attending a public or private school and wish to get an idea of your general academic achievement you may sign up for private testing through one of the home school testing services.

### Career Interest Surveys
Career interest inventories are given and interpreted to high school students in the career centers of high-schools or at community colleges. These tests will help you identify your areas of strong interest and lists career possibilities related to interests.

ASVAB (Armed Services Vocational Aptitude Battery), and CAPS (Career Ability Placement Survey) are also available in your local high school or community college career centers.

You may also take "Interest Surveys" at home with programs such as CareerPath. See Section I for more details.

### College Tests
There are two national tests and one state test which are used for college admission and/or placement. Although some generalizations can be made, it is impossible to be specific about which colleges require which tests. Students should always check the college catalog

to make sure which tests are required or recommended by the colleges they wish to attend. This information is also available in *Barron's Profiles of American Colleges, Lovejoy's College Guide*, and *Peterson's College Guide*. The three testing programs are the College Entrance Examination Board (CEEB), the American College Testing Program (ACT), and Washington Pre-College (WPC). Applications for these tests are available in the counselor's office or career center of your local high-school.

The following is a brief description of what each of these tests measure:

**1) CEEB** (College Entrance Examination Board) has four elements:

PSAT/NMSQT (Preliminary Scholastic Aptitude Test/National Merit Scholarship Qualifying Test). These are combined into one test which is given only once a year during October. Juniors are strongly encouraged to take the exam. This exam is for the following purposes:

• Giving students practice for and some indication of how well they will do on the SAT or College Board test.

• Screening for the selection of finalists for the National Merit Scholarship Program.

• Enabling students to draw some comparisons between their math and verbal skills to allow them to strengthen areas of weakness in their senior year.

• Beginning early and realistic planning of college choice.

SAT (Scholastic Aptitude Test), is also now labeled ATP (Admission Testing Program. The SAT is often called the "College Board." It is a three-hour objective test designed to measure how well students have developed their verbal and mathematical skills. The SAT is required for admission and placement at many colleges throughout the United States. The test is given several times each year. The best time to take the test is in the spring of the junior year or early fall of the senior year. Results are mailed to the student's home, high-school, and specified colleges and universities. The first major change in the SAT, since it was begun in 1926, occurred in 1994. The new SAT (called SAT II) places greater emphasis on critical reading and writing. There are more "story problems" in the Mathematics section. If you plan to use a SAT preparation text, make sure it is for the SAT II or is newer than 1994. Used or discounted out-of-date copies will be no bargain. For test dates and locations you may write the College Board.

ACH (Achievement Tests) one-hour tests designed to measure a student's level of achievement in a particular subject. Achievement tests are given in such academic subjects as English, Science, Math, and Foreign Languages. Students should consult college catalogs to see if these exams are required and which test date is preferred. The tests are given on the same dates as the SAT; however, both tests cannot be taken the same day. Results are mailed to the home, high-school, and specified colleges and universities.

AP (Advanced Placement Exam) may be taken in any subject for possible college credit and provides a means by which secondary school students may demonstrate their readiness to take advanced courses as college freshman. If the student's college grants academic credit for the AP examination, there will be fewer credits for the student to complete for graduation, possibly saving both time and tuition fees. AP tests are given in May. Each local high-school offers different AP courses and tests. Ask your local high-school counselors for information regarding which tests their school offers. You may be able to prepare for more than one test by taking the tests offered at different schools. Write to the College Board at Box 886, New York, New York 10101-0886 for information on which tests are offered. Results of these tests are mailed to your home, the school where you sat for the examination, and to specified colleges and universities.

2) ACT (American College Testing Program)

is a measure of scholastic aptitude in English, mathematics, social studies, and natural sciences required for admission and placement by some colleges. Seniors should register to retake the ACT in the fall and not hesitate to retake the test in order to improve your score. Results are sent to the high-school you took the test through, colleges, and universities.

3) WPC (Washington Pre-College) Testing Program is a comprehensive career guidance tool for Washington students which also is used for admissions and placement purposes by colleges and universities in this and nearby states. Although the WPC is given in both the Spring (for Juniors) and the Fall (as a make-up for Seniors), students should plan to take it in the Spring of their Junior year if possible. This will assure them of having the results in time for early college applications and will give them a better opportunity to use the materials for academic and/or career planning. Students should check with their counselor or career center for testing dates and fee information.

## Community College Testing

The ASSET is a survey and a set of short tests given to students enrolling into community colleges throughout the United States. (It is also the examination used to determine a student's eligibility for Project Running Start, an early entry program for high-school students. See Paying For College section for complete description). Students give details about their past schools and about their future plans. ASSET then tests the basic skills needed to succeed in community college. ASSET is now used by many community colleges for admissions testing and is needed for acceptance for Project Running Start. The ASSET test is useful for advising students entering community college programs. The test takes about two and a half to three hours to complete. The Testing Center at your community college gives ASSET tests in small groups at frequent intervals. It is free. Results are generally available the next day. Contact your local community college for information and testing times.

G.E.D. (General Education Development) also known as the "high-school equivalency test" is administered to students who do not wish to worry about earning a specified number of credits and who are planning to enter directly into the military, work place, or attend community college or a vocational school.

Some colleges and universities may require the G.E.D. Test of home schooled students wishing to enter their schools, especially schools located in states where home schooling is not common. A student must be 19 years old or older to take the examination without the approval of the local school district. Many local school districts have been cooperative with home schoolers in granting approval for testing for student between 16 and 19 years old. The regulations for G.E.D. testing vary with each state's charter. For example, in Washington State, students who are registered as home schoolers may take the G.E.D. without school district approval beginning at age 16. If this applies to you, you may contact the Department of Public Instruction for an application form or for more information. Special preparatory classes for the tests are available at community colleges and vocational schools. The test is administered at most community colleges and vocational schools on a regular basis.

# Appendix C

## Suggested Reading Material

### College Planning Resources

*50 College Admission Directors Speak to Parents*, 1988.

*Bear's Guide to Earning Non-Traditional College Degrees*, John Bear, 1990.

*Campus-Free College Degrees: Thorson's complete guide to accredited off-campus college degree programs.* 1989.

*Campus Visits and College Interviews*, Zola Schneider, 1987.

*Choosing a College: A Guide for Parents and Students*, Thomas Sowell, Conservative Book Club, 1989. This hard to find volume gives a clear look at American Colleges. Candid reports of the admissions, campus life, and academic world. The information on "campus life" is unique - it tells you such things as the college's attitude to co-ed dorms and overnight visitors, etc. Try to locate it from your library or through interlibrary loan.

*Contests for Students*, Mary Ellen Snodgrass, editor, Gale Research, Inc. 1991, Detroit. Over 600 contest and competitions which preschoolers through college students can enter to earn scholarships and academic recognition. Excellent for preparing for college; includes age index, prize index, subject and type of competition index; Prize index and sponsoring organization index.

*College Blue Book: Scholarships, Fellowships, Grants, and Loans*, 1989. General guide to financial aid sources for all levels of postsecondary education. Provides information by level of education being sought and by academic major.

*College Degrees by Mail,* Dr. John Bear, Ten Speed Press, Updated annually. Mary Pride says: "Buy this Book!!!" She claims it is the ultimate book for those who would like to earn a degree by mail.

*Composing a Successful Application Essay: Write your way into College*, George Ehrenhaft, 1987.

*Earn & Learn: Cooperative education opportunities offered by the federal government.* A guide to combining work opportunities with classroom instruction.

*Financing a College Education: The Essential Guide for the 90s*, Judith B. Margolin, Plenum Press, 1990, New York. A book, clearly written for parents and students, gives complete explanations of the student loan process, grants and scholarships. Explains ways to reduce cost of college as well as work study options.

*Fiske Guide to Colleges*, Edward B. Fiske, 1989.

*Free Money for College*, Laurie Blum, Facts on File, 1990, New York. Four categories of sources for college money geographic listing, subject listing, special groups (ethnic, religious, etc.), and more. Also included grants for members of groups, employees or their dependents, etc. Good resource.

*Home Study Opportunities: The Complete Guide to going to college by Mail*, Laurie M. Carlson, Betterway Books, 1989. Gives information on earning high school and college diplomas by mail. Detailed school and program listings.

*How to Build a College Fund for Your Child*, Paine Weber, 1989.

*How to Get Into the Right College, Secrets of college admissions officers*, Edward B. Fiske, 1988.

*How to Pay for Your Children's College Education*, Gerald Krefetz, 1988.

*Independent Study Catalog*, NUCEA's guide to Independent study through correspondence instruction. 1989.

*Lovejoy's College Guide*, published annually.

*National Review College Guide*, Charles Sykes and Brad Miner, editors, Wolgemuth and Hyatt Publishers, 1991. Describes colleges that focus on a traditional liberal arts program. (Liberal in the "classical" academic sense.) Great resources for conservative families.

*Pacific Northwest Scholarship Options Guide.* College Planning Network, 1990, Seattle, WA. Lists specific scholarships, grants , and loan programs only available to students who are residents of the Pacific Northwest. Excellent resource for little known (less competitive) scholarships.

*Putting Your Kids Through College*, Scott Edelstein, 1989.

## Information On Home Schooling
*The Home School Manual*, 5th Edition. By Theodore E. Wade, Jr. and others. Gazelle Publications, 1994. This book includes list of topics usually covered in each subject by grade as well as an article on home schooling teenagers.

*High School Curriculum Manual*, Cathy Duffy, Home Run Enterprises, 1995. Excellent resource for families home schooling during the high school years. Reviews curriculum as well as describes in detail options for home schooling.

## Visit these web sites:
http://www.changes-in-attitud.com/changes/educat/tuition

http://www.armory.com/~jon/hs/spice.html#college

## Money Making and Management
*The Teen Age Liberation Handbook*

*Capitalism for Kids: Growing Up To Be Your Own Boss,* Karl Hess, Dearborn Publishing, 1987. Book explains how to create your own job and gives examples of young people who have done it successfully.

*Monthly Money: Allowance & Responsibility System For Kids and Teenagers*, Complete money management system for young people. 1994

*How to Become a Teenage Millionaire*, Todd Temple, Thomas Nelson Publishers, Nashville, TN.

## Study Skills & Learning Styles
*More Than a Grade! Learning That Lasts a Lifetime*, Cynthia Ulrich Tobias, M.Ed. This program helps you determine your learning style. Learning Styles Unlimited, Inc., 31919 First Ave. South, Suite 243, Federal Way, WA. 98003

*You Are Smarter Than You Think! A Practical Guide To Academic Success Using Your Personal Learning Style,* Renee Mollan-Masters, M.A. Reality Productions, 1992.

## Choosing A Career
*Careers without College: No B.S. Necessary,* JoAnn Russo, Blue Stocking Press, looks at ten open-ended careers you can get into without a college degree. Great Resource.

*CareerPath: Career Exploration and Guidance Software*, Ontrack Media, 1995. This program allows you to complete an interest survey to narrow down you potential areas of interest. It gives a list of related jobs. You can then look in the directory of careers to determine more details about the job, for example educational requirements, pay scale and so on. It also provides information on time management and job application. And one of the best things of all is the answers you get are on your own computer, guaranteeing no danger of exploitation of "private" information.

# Appendix D
# Contact Resources
## State Home School Support Groups

—AK—

Alaska Home School Network
PO Box 878887
Wasilla AK 99687
907/892-8017

Alaska Homeschool Assn
PO Box 874075
Wasilla AK 99687
907/373-7404

Alaska Private & Home Ed. Assn
PO Box 141764
Anchorage AK 99514
907-696-0641

—AL—

Alabama Home Educators
PO Box 16091
Mobile AL 36116

Fellowship of Christian Home Ed.
PO Box 563
Alabaster AL 35007
205/664-2232

—AR—

Arkansas Christian Home Educators Assn
PO Box 4025
N Little Rock AR 72190
501/758-9099

—AZ—

Arizona Families for Home Education
PO Box 4661
Scottsdale AZ 85261-4661
602/276-8548

Parents Assn of Christian Home Sch.
6166 W Highland
Phoenix AZ 85033

—CA—

California Homeschool Network
PO Box 44
Vineburg CA 95487-0044
1-800-327-5339

C.H. E. A. of Calif. (Christian)
PO Box 2009
Norwalk CA 90651-2009
310-864-2432

CHECK (Catholic)
115 West California Blvd. #133
Pasadena, CA. 91105
818-441-7714

Home School Association of California
PO Box 2442
Atascadero CA 93423
805-462-0726

—CO—

Catholic Home Educators of Colorado
652 S Alcott St
Denver CO 80219

Christian Home Educators of CO
3739 E 4th Ave
Denver CO 80206-1237
303-388-1888

Colorado Home Educators Assn
1616 17th St
Denver CO 80209
303-441-9938

Colorado Home Schooling Network
7490 W Apache
Sedalia CO 80135
303/688-4136

Concerned Parents for Colorado
PO Box 547
Florissant CO 80816-0547

St. Joseph's Catholic H. S. Group
1709 C Spring Meadows Ct.
Ft. Collins, CO. 80525
303/ 482-4755

—CT—

Connecticut Home Educators Assn
1590 N Benson Rd
Fairfield CT 06430

Connecticut Home Schooler Assn
98 Bahe Rd
Deep River CT 04101

T.E.A.C.H. (Christian)
25 Field Stone Run
Farmington CT 06032
203-243-3830

—DC—

Bolling Area Home Schoolers of DC
1419A Wright Circle
Bolling AFB DC 20336

—DE—

Delaware Home Education Assn
51 Michaelangelo Ct
Hockessin DE 19707
302-998-6194

—FL—

Florida at Home
4644 Adanson
Orlando FL 32804
407-740-8877

Florida Parent Educators Association
PO Box 1193
Venice FL 34284-1193
941-492-6938

Gulf Coast Christian Home Ed. Assn
PO Box 86
Mary Esther FL 32569
904-729-7881

—GA—

Apostolate for Catholic Home Ed.
Dr. & Mrs. Joseph Burnette
2805 Willcox Ct.
Albany, GA. 31707

Catholic Home Educators of Georgia
74 Williamson St.
Jefferson, GA 30549
706/ 367-2437

Georgia Home Education Association
245 Buckeye Lane
Fayetteville GA 30214
404-461-3657

North Georgia Home School Assn
200 W Crest Rd
Rossville GA 30741
706-861-1795

Georgians For Freedom in Ed.
7180 Cane Leaf Drive
Fairburn, GA 30213
770/463-1563

**—HI—**

Christian Homeschoolers of Hawaii
91-284 Oama St
Ewa Beach HI 96706
808/674-1335

Hawaii Home School Assn
PO Box 3476
Mililani HI 96789
808-625-0445

Hawaii Island Christian Home Ed.
614 Hoomalu Pl
Hilo HI 96793

Hawaii Island Home Educators
PO Box 851
Mountain View HI 96771-0851
808/968-8076

**—IA—**

Iowa Families for Christian Education
RR 3 Box 143
Missouri Valley IA 51555

Iowa Home Educators Assn
PO Box 213
Des Moines IA 50301-0213
515/262-9088

Iowa Home Educators Assn
818 N Utah Ave
Davenport IA 52804
319-323-3735

Network of Iowa Christian Home Ed.
PO Box 158
Dexter IA 50070
515-830-1514

**—ID—**

Home Educators of Idaho
3618 Pine Hill Dr
Coeur d'Alene ID 83814
208/667-2778

Idaho Home Educators
PO Box 4022
Boise ID 83711
208/482-7336

**—IL—**

Christian Home Educators Coalition
PO Box 470322
Chicago IL 60647
312/278-0673

Illinois Christian Home Educators
PO Box 261
Zion IL 60099-0261
847/662-1909

Southern Illinois Christian Home Ed.
1612 Isabella
Mt Vernon IL 62864
618-242-1324

**—IN—**

Central Indiana Home Educators
7262 Lakeside Dr
Indianapolis IN 46278

Indiana Association of Home Ed.
PO Box 1051
Noblesville IN 46060
317-770-0644

**—KS—**

Christian Home Educators Assn
PO Box 3968
Wichita KS 67201
913-234-2927

**—KY—**

Christian Home Ed. of Kentucky
691 Howardstown Rd
Hodgenville KY 42748
502/358-9270

Kentucky Christian H. S.I Assn
1301 Bridget Dr
Fairdale KY 40118
502/363-5194

Kentucky Home Ed. Assn
PO Box 81
Winchester KY 40392-0081
606/744-8562

Midwest Catholic Home Ed. Assoc.
618 Washington
Covington, KY 41011
606/ 431-7059

**—LA—**

CHEF of Louisiana
PO Box 74292
Baton Rouge LA 70874-4292
504/775-9709

Louisiana Citizens for Home Ed.
3404 Van Buren
Baker LA 70714
504/775-5472

**—MA—**

Massachusetts Home Learning Assn
16 Anderson Rd
Marlboro MA 01752
508/485-3765

Massachusetts HOPE
15 Ohio St
Wilmington MA 01887
508/658-8970

**—MD—**

Christian Home Educators Network
2826 Roselawn Ave
Baltimore MD 21214
410-444-5465

Maryland Assn of Christian Home Ed.
PO Box 3964
Frederick MD 21701
301/663-3999

Maryland Home Education Assn
9085 Flamepool Way
Columbia MD 21045
301/730-0073

Parents for Home Education
13020 Blairmore St
Beltsville MD 20705
301/572-5827

**—ME—**

Homeschoolers of Maine
HC 62 Box 24
Hope ME 04847
207-763-4251
Fax: 207-763-4352

Maine Homeschool Assn
PO Box 587
Unity ME 04988-0587
207/777-1700

**—MI—**

Christian Home Ed. of Michigan
PO Box 2357
Farmington Hills MI 48333
810-683-3395
Fax: 810-978-2808

CHURCH (Catholic)
Greater Lansing Area, MI
517/ 349-5314

Network for Christian Homes
4934 Cannonsburg Rd
Belmont MI 49306-9614
616-874-5656

**—MN—**

MN Assn of Christian Home Ed.
PO Box 188
Anoka MN 55303
612/617-9070

Minnesota Assn. of RC Home Ed
7211 Sherwood Echo
Woodbury MN 55125
612-730-8101

Minnesota Home School Network
9669 E 123rd
Hastings MN 55033
612/437-3049

Minnesota Home Schoolers Alliance
1603 1st Ave S
Anoka MN 55303
612-427-6746

— MO—

Christian Home Educators Fellowship
1344 N Bend Rd
Union MO 63084

Families for Home Education
400 E High Point Ln
Columbia MO 65203

MO Assoc Teaching Christian Homes
307 East Ash Street #146
Columbia MO 65201
314-443-2506

— MS—

Home Educators of Southern MS
1108 Post Rd
Clinton MS 39056
601-924-3697

Mississippi Home Educators Assn
109 Reagan Ranch Rd
Laurel MS 39440
601-649-6432

Mississippi H. S. Support Group
21550 Darling Rd
Pass Christian MS 39571

— MT—

Montana Coalition of Home Educators
PO Box 654
Helena MT 59624

Montana Home Education
1510 Longhorn Way
Billings MT 59105
406-273-6860

Montana Homeschoolers Assn
PO Box 95
Ulm MT 59485-0095

— NC—

Home Education Assn
300 Brown Circle
Rolesville NC 27571
919-554-1563

North Carolinians for Home Ed.
419 N Boylan Ave
Raleigh NC 27603-1211
919-834-6243

— ND—

North Dakota Home School Assn
PO Box 486
Mandan ND 58554
701/663-2868

North Dakota Home School Assn
4007 N State St
Bismarck ND 58501
701-223-4080

— NE—

Nebraska Christian H E A
PO Box 57041
Lincoln NE 68505-7041
402-423-4297

Nebraska Independent H.S. Network
8010 Lillibridge St
Lincoln NE 68506

— NH—

N.H. Alliance for Home Education
16 Winter Cir RFD 3
Manchester NH 03103

New Hampshire H. S.I Coalition
PO Box 2224
Concord NH 03301

— NJ—

NJ Family Schools Assn
RD 3 Box 208
Washington NJ 07882

Unschoolers Network
2 Smith St
Farmingdale NJ 07727
908/938-2473

— NM—

New Mexico Christian Home Ed.
5749 Paradise Blvd NW
Albuquerque NM 87114
505/897-1772

NM Family Home Educators
5018 Cordoniz NW
Albuquerque NM 87120
505-899-0652

— NV—

Christian Home Educators of Nevada
1011 Sagerock Way
North Las Vegas NV 89301

— NY—

Home Education Network of NY
2933 Clover St
Pittsford NY 14534
716-381-9279

Loving Education at Home
PO Box 88
Cato NY 13033-0088

— OH—

Association of Ohio Homeschoolers
748 Sheridan Ave
Columbus OH 43209
614-237-7624

Christian Home Educators of Ohio
PO Box 1224
Kent OH 44240
614-474-3177

— OK—

Christian Home Educators Fellowship
PO Box 471363
Tulsa OK 74147
918/583-7323

Oklahoma Central Home Educators
PO Box 270601
Oklahoma City OK 73137
405/521-8439

— OR—

Oregon Christian Home Ed. Assn
2515 NE 37th
Portland OR 97212
503/288-1285

Parents Education Assn
PO Box 5428
Aloha OR 97006-0428

— PA—

Christian Home Education Assn
2200 Huber Dr
Manheim PA 17545-9130
717/653-8892

Christian H.S. Association of PA
PO Box 3603
York PA 17402
717-661-2428

Home Educators of Pennsylvania
Rt 2 Box 334-A
Munson PA 16860
814/345-6273

Pennsylvania Home Ed. Network
1003 Arborwood Dr
Gibsonia PA 15044
412-443-5114

Rhode Island Guild of Home Teachers
272 Pequot Ave
Warwick RI 02886
401/737-2265

Rhode Islanders Constitutional Ed.
1 Solar St
Providence RI 02903
401/861-9685

**—SC—**

Carolina Family School Assn
162 Fox Run Ln
Columbia SC 29210-4970

Catholic Home Educators of SC
1570 Huntsman Dr
Aiken SC 29803
803-649-6367

SC Assn of Independent H. S.
PO Box 2104
Irmo SC 29063
803/732-8680

South Carolina Home Ed. Assn
506 Tracy Trail
Green SC 29651
803-234-0603

South Carolina Home Ed. Assn.
PO Box 612
Lexington SC 29071
803-951-8960

**—SD—**

South Dakota Home School Assn
PO Box 882
Sioux Falls SD 57101

Western Dakota Christian H. S.
PO Box 528
Black Hawk SD 57718-0528
605-787-4153

**—TN—**

Tennessee Home Education Assn
3677 Richbriar Ct
Nashville TN 37211
615/834-3529

West Tennessee Home Ed.Assn
246 Ramblewood Dr
Jackson TN 38305-1853
901-664-6740

**—TX—**

Home Oriented Private Ed. for Texas
PO Box 59876
Dallas TX 75229-1876
214-358-2221

Southeast Texas Home School Assn
4950 FM 1960 #C3-87
Houston TX 77069
713/370-8787

Texas Home School Coalition
PO Box 6982
Lubbock TX 79493
806-797-4927

**—UT—**

Utah Christian Homeschoolers
PO Box 3942
Salt Lake City UT 84110-3942
801/774-8748

Utah Home Education Assn
PO Box 50565
Provo UT 84605-0565
801-535-1533

**—VA—**

HEA of Virginia
PO Box 1810
Front Royal VA 22630-1810
703/635-9322

Our Lady of Good Counsel Chpt.
1130 Castle Hollow Road
Midlothian, VA 23113
804/ 741-4053 (Mary Jane)
804/ 794-5374 (Yvonne)

Virginia Home Education Assn
Rt 1 Box 370
Gordonsville VA 22942
703-832-3578

**—VT—**

Christian Home Ed. of Vermont
2 Webster Avenue
Barre VT 05641-4818
802-476-8821

Vermont Catholics United for Ed.
17 Lindale Dr
Colchester VT 05446
802-878-0843

Vermont Home Schoolers Assn
Rt 1 Box 6680
Middletown Springs VT 05757
802/235-2620

Vermont Home Schoolers Assn
PO Box 161
Pittsford VT 05763
802/483-6296

**—WA—**

Family Learning Organization of WA
PO Box 7256
Spokane WA 99207-0256
509/467-2552

ST. Thomas More Home Educators
3853 76th Ave. S.E.
Mercer Island, WA 98040-3441
206/230-0455

WATCH (Christian)
PO Box 980
Airway Heights WA 99001-0980
509/299-3766

WHO (inclusive)
18130 Midvale Ave N #C
Seattle WA 98133
206/546-9438

**—WI—**

Families in Schools at Home
4639 Conestoga Trail
Cottage Grove WI 53527

Holy Family Homeschool Group
412 Whipple Tree Lane
Waterford, WI 53185
414/ 534-4977

N.W. Wisconsin Catholic H. S.
701 Mollies Way
De Pere WI 54115
802-878-0843

Wisconsin Christian Home Ed.
2307 Carmel Ave
Racine WI 53405
414/657-5127

Wisconsin Parents Assn.
PO Box 2502
Madison WI 53701

**—WV—**

Christian Home Educators of WV
PO Box 8770
South Charleston WV 25303
304-776-4664

West Virginia Home Educators Assn
PO Box 7504
Charleston WV 25356

**—WY—**

Home Schoolers of Wyoming
PO Box 926
Evansville WY 82636-0926
307-745-3536

Homeschoolers of Wyoming
339 Bicentennial Ct
Powell WY 82435
307-754-3271

Unschoolers of Wyoming
429 Hwy 230 #20
Laramie WY 82070

Wyoming Homeschoolers
PO Box 1386
Lyman WY 82937
307/787-6728

# State Departments of Education

Warning. It is advised that you double-check all information provided by the following sources with your local or state home school support group. Some home school families claim to have received conflicting, confusing, and/or erroneous information from their State Department of Education personnel. This information is provided primarily to facilitate any request for necessary documents or forms.

Alabama Department of Education
Room 483, State Office Building
Montgomery, AL 36130
(205) 261-5156

Alaska Department of Education
Pouch F
Juneau, AK 99811
(907) 465-2800

Arizona Department of Education
1535 West Jefferson
Phoenix, AZ 85007
(602) 255-5057

Arkansas Department of Education
Educ. Bldg., 4 State Capitol Mall
Little Rock, AR 72201-1020
(501) 371-1461

California Department of Education
721 Capitol Mall, Room 524
Sacramento, CA. 95814
(916) 445-4338

Colorado Department of Education
201 East Colfax Avenue
Denver, CO. 80203.
(303) 866-6806

Connecticut Dept. of Education
165 Capitol Avenue
Hartford, CT. 06106
(203) 566-5061

Delaware Dept. of Public Instr.
Townsend Building
Dover, DE. 19901
(302) 736-4602

D.C. Public Schools
415 12th St. NW
Washington D.C. 20004
(202) 724-4222

Florida Department of Education
The Capitol
Tallahassee, FL. 32301
(904) 487-1785

Georgia Department of Education
205 Butler Street Southeast
Atlanta, GA 30334
(404) 656-2800

Hawaii Department of Education
Office of Instructional Services
Student Personnel Services Section
941 Hind Luka Drive
Honolulu, HI 96821
(808) 548-6583

Idaho Department of Education
Len B. Jordan Building
650 West State Street
Boise, ID 83720
(208) 334-3300

Illinois State Board of Education
100 North First Street
Springfield, IL 62777
(217) 782-2221

Indiana Dept. of Public Instruction
227 State House
Indianapolis, IN 46204
(317) 232-6667

Iowa Dept. of Public Instruction
Grimes State Office Building
Des Moines, IA 50319
(515) 281-5294

Kansas Department of Education
120 East 10th Street
Topeka, KS 66612
(913) 296-3201

Kentucky Dept. of Education
Capital Plaza Tower
Frankfort, KY 40601
(502) 564-4770

Louisiana Department of Education
P.O. Box 94064
Baton Rouge, LA 70804-9064
(504) 342-3602

Maine Dept. of Ed. Services
State House Station #23
Augusta, ME 04333
(207) 289-5802

Maryland Dept. of Education
200 West Baltimore Street
Baltimore, MD 21201
(301) 659-2100

Massachusetts Dept. of Education
1385 Hancock Street
Quincy, MA 02169
(617) 770-7300

Michigan Department of Education
520 Michigan National Tower
P.O. Box 30008
Lansing, MI 48909
(517) 373-3354

Minnesota Department of Educ.
550 Cedar Street, 8th Floor
St. Paul, MN 55101
(612) 296-2358

Mississippi Department of Educ.
501 Sillers Building
Jackson, MS 39201
(601) 359-3513

Missouri Dept. of Education
515 East High Street, Box 480
Jefferson City, MO 65102
(314) 751-4446

Montana Office of Public Instr.
State Capitol
Helena, MT 59620
(406) 444-3654

Nebraska Dept. of Education
301 Centennial Mall South
P.O. Box 94987
Lincoln, NE 68509-4987
(402) 471-2465

Nevada Department of Education
400 West King Street
Carson City, NV 89710
(702) 885-3100

New Hampshire Dept. of Education
State Office Park South
Concord, NH 03301
(603) 271-3144

New Jersey Dept. of Education
225 West State Street
Trenton, NJ 08625
(609) 292-4450

New Mexico Department of Education
Education Building
Santa Fe, NM 87501-2786
(505) 827-6635

New York Dept. of Education
Education Building
Albany, NY 12234
(518) 474-5844

North Carolina Dept. of Education
Governor's Office for Non-Public Ed.
116 West Edenton Street
Raleigh, NC 27603-1712
(919) 733-3813

North Dakota Dept. of Instruction
11th Floor, State Capitol
Bismarck, ND 58505
(701) 224-2261

For High School:
North Dakota Dept. of Instruction
Division of Independent Study
Box 5036, State University Station
Fargo, ND 58105
(701) 237-7182

Ohio Department of Education
65 S. Front Street, Room 808
Columbus, OH 43215
(614) 466-3304

Oklahoma Dept. of Education
2500 North Lincoln Blvd.
Oklahoma City, OK 73105
(405) 521-3301

Oregon Department of Education
700 Pringle Parkway Southeast
Salem, OR 97310
(503) 378-3573

Pennsylvania Dept. of Education
10th Floor, Harristown Building #2
Harrisburg, PA. 17108
(717) 787-5820

Rhode Island Department of Education
22 Hayes Street
Providence, RI 02908
(401) 277-2031

South Carolina Dept. of Education
Rutledge Building
1429 Senate Street
Columbia, SC 29201
(803 734-8458

South Dakota Dept of Education
Kneip Building
Pierre, SD 57501
(605) 773-3243

Tennessee Dept. of Education
100 Cordell Hull Building
Nashville, TN 37219
(615) 741-2731

Texas Education Agency
201 East 11th Street
Austin, TX 78701
(512) 834-4000

Utah Office of Education
250 East Fifth Street South
Salt Lake City, UT 84111
(801) 538-7743

Vermont Department of Education
120 State Street
Montpelier, VT 05602
(802) 828-3135

Virginia Department of Education
P.O. Box 6-Q
Richmond, VA 23216
(804) 225-2023

Washington Supt. of Instruction
Office of Private Education
Old Capitol Building FG-11
Olympia, WA 98504-3211
(360) 753-6717

West Virginia Dept. of Education
1800 Washington Street East, Building 6
Charleston, WV 25305
(304) 348- 2681

Wisconsin Dept. of Public Instruction
125 South Webster Street
P.O. Box 7841
Madison, WI 53707
(608) 266-1771

Wyoming Dept. of Education
Hathaway Building
Cheyenne, WY 82002
(307) 777-7675

# Home School Suppliers

21st Century Education Resources
4248 Chicago Rd
Warren MI 48092
810-978-2808
Fax: 810-978-9293

Academy Supplies
17000 W Valley Hwy
Tukwila WA 98188
206-251-0574
Fax: 206-251-0128
1-800-275-7068

Atco School Supply
PO Box 1707
Corona CA 91718-1707
909-272-2926
Fax: 909-272-3457

Bearly Used Books
N 2904 Dora Rd
Spokane WA 99212-1518
509/922-4811

Betterway Christian Book Store
5455 N Henry Blvd
Stockbridge GA 30281

Builder Books
PO Box 5291
Lynnwood WA 98046-5291
206/778-4526

Castlemoyle Books
15436 32nd Ave S
Seattle WA 98188
Fax: 206/244-5382
Toll Free:1-888-SPELL TOO

Children's Books
PO Box 19069
Denver CO 80219
303-237-4989
Fax: 303-433-6788

Christian Life Workshops
PO Box 2250
Gresham OR 97030
503-667-3942
Fax: 503-665-6637

Christian Supply Center Inc.
10209 SE Division St
Portland OR 97266
503-251-1590
Fax: 503-255-7690
1-800-929-0683

Chula Vista Books
420 Chula Vista Mtn Rd
Pell City AL 35125
205-338-1843

Creative Home Teaching
PO Box 152581
San Diego CA 92195
619-263-8633
Fax: 619-263-8633

The Drinking Gourd
PO Box 2557
Redmond WA 98073
206/836-0336
Fax: 206/868-1371
1-800-TDG-5487

Eagle's Nest
1539 Oakwood Dr
Escala CA 95320
209-838-3193
Fax: 209-838-6747

Education Plus
PO Box 1029
Mauldin SC 29662
864-281-9316
Fax: 864-458-7257

The Education Supply House
Rt 1 Box 541
Martinsville IL 62442

Emeth Educational Supplies
20618 Cyprus Way
Lynnwood WA 98036
206/672-8708

Exodus Multimedia Services
19144-A Molalla Ave
Oregon City OR 97045
503/655-1951

Family Learning Exchange
Olympia WA
360-438-1865

Farm Country General Store
Rt 1 Box 63
Metamora IL 61548
309/367-2844
Fax: 309-367-2844
1-800-551-FARM

Gateway Curriculum Center
PO Box 20111
Memphis TN 38168
901-454-0646

Greenleaf Press
1570 Old LaGuardo Rd
Lebanon TN 37087
615-449-1617
Fax: 615/449-4018

HIS Publishing
1732 NE 3rd Ave
Ft. Lauderdale FL 33305
305-764-4567

Home Education Center
487 Myatt Dr
Madison TN 37115
615-860-3000

Home Learning Center
1020 Helena Flats
Kalispell MT 59901-6623
406/755-4542

Home School Book & Bible Store
4742 Barnes Road
Colorado Springs CO 80917
719-574-4222

The Home School Books & Supplies
104 S West Ave
Arlington WA 98223
206-435-0376
Fax: 206/435-1028
1-800-788-1221

Home School Supply House
PO Box 2000
Beaver UT 84713-2000
801/438-1254
1-800-772-3129

Home Schooling at its Best
23923 SE 202nd St
Maple Valley WA 98038
206/432-9805

Honey Tree Educational Supply
3110 Biddle Rd
Bellville OH 44813-9237
419-886-4462

Honeycomb Instructional Materials
17919 NW 41st Ave
Ridgefield WA 98642
360-573-0798

J.W. Books
Tukwila WA 98188
206/246-1435

Kadlac Design
10601 Douglas Dr
Brooklyn Park MN 55443
612/424-8373

Learning Lights
PO Box 40875
Eugene OR 97404
503-935-6024

Learning Safari
3463 E Kolonels Way
Pt Angeles WA 98362
360/452-5045

Lifetime Books and Gifts
3900 Chalet Suzanne Dr
Lake Wales FL 33853-7763
941-676-6311
Fax: 941-676-1814
1-800-377-0390

Master Enterprises Lrng Ctr
8323 95th St SW
Tacoma WA 98498
206/581-1588
Fax: 206/584-1011

Rainbow Re-Source Center
8227 Ulah Rd
Cambridge IL 61238
309-937-3385
Fax: 309-937-3382

School Works
609 8th St SE
Auburn WA 98002
206/735-3642

Shekinah Curriculum Bookstore
101 Meador Rd
Kilgore TX 75662
903-643-2796
Fax: 903-643-2796

Sonshine Learning Center
15916 56th Ave Ct E
Puyallup WA 98373
206/537-8120

St Michael The Archangel Academy
Irvine CA 92720
714/730-9114

Whiz Kids
N 5628 Division St
Spokane WA 99207
509/483-9153

# Appendix E

## Forms Described in This Text

Important! Do not write on the original forms that follow. (Originals are those bound in this book.) Make the number of copies suggested on the list below:

| .Form Description | Number of sides | Number of Copies |
|---|---|---|
| Attendance Record Sheet | 1 side | 1 |
| Personal Data Sheet | 2 sides | 1 |
| Life Goals Sheet | 2 sides | 1 |
| Dates to Remember | 2 sides | 1 |
| Commemorative Days and Holidays | 2 sides | 1 |
| 1996-1997 School Year | 2 sides | 1 |
| 1997-1998 School Year | 2 sides | 1 |
| 1998-1999 School Year | 2 sides | 1 |
| 1999-2000 School Year | 2 sides | 1 |
| 2000-2001 School Year | 2 sides | 1 |
| Month of _____ | 2 sides | 12 per year |
| Tentative High School Plan | 4 sides | 1 |
| Freshman Year Plan | 2 sides | 1 |
| Sophomore Year Plan | 2 sides | 1 |
| Junior Year Plan | 2 sides | 1 |
| Senior Year Plan | 2 sides | 1 |
| Course Planning Sheet | 2 sides | 1 for each course (6-24) |
| Course Requirement Sheet | 2 sides | 1 for each course (6-24) |
| Project-Report Grading Forms | 2 sides | As needed (10) |
| Essay-Composition Forms | 2 sides | As needed (10) |
| Project Planning Sheet | 2 sides | As needed (10) |
| Week Goal/Priority List | 2 sides | 52* |
| Weekly Schedule | 6 sides | 52* |
| Course Record Sheet | 2 sides | 1 for each course (6-24) |
| Transcript/Report Card | 2 sides | 4 |
| Reading Record | 2 sides | As Needed (10) |
| Summary of Experiences | 2 sided | 1 |
| Experience Record | 2 sides | As Needed (10) |
| Scholarship/Bond Summary | 2 sides | 1 |
| Income / Expenses for _____ | 1 side | 12 |
| Summary of Income / Expenses | 1 side | 1 |

* You may want to make only one set of these forms until you have completed the exercises at the end of Section VI.

# Attendance History

Student Name: _____ Year: _____

| | 1 | 2 | 3 | 4 | 5 | 6 | 7 | 8 | 9 | 10 | 11 | 12 | 13 | 14 | 15 | 16 | 17 | 18 | 19 | 20 | 21 | 22 | 23 | 24 | 25 | 26 | 27 | 28 | 29 | 30 | 31 |
|---|---|---|---|---|---|---|---|---|---|---|---|---|---|---|---|---|---|---|---|---|---|---|---|---|---|---|---|---|---|---|---|
| Sept | | | | | | | | | | | | | | | | | | | | | | | | | | | | | | | |
| Oct | | | | | | | | | | | | | | | | | | | | | | | | | | | | | | | |
| Nov | | | | | | | | | | | | | | | | | | | | | | | | | | | | | | | |
| Dec | | | | | | | | | | | | | | | | | | | | | | | | | | | | | | | |
| Jan | | | | | | | | | | | | | | | | | | | | | | | | | | | | | | | |
| Feb | | | | | | | | | | | | | | | | | | | | | | | | | | | | | | | |
| Mar | | | | | | | | | | | | | | | | | | | | | | | | | | | | | | | |
| Apr | | | | | | | | | | | | | | | | | | | | | | | | | | | | | | | |
| May | | | | | | | | | | | | | | | | | | | | | | | | | | | | | | | |
| Jun | | | | | | | | | | | | | | | | | | | | | | | | | | | | | | | |
| Jul | | | | | | | | | | | | | | | | | | | | | | | | | | | | | | | |
| Aug | | | | | | | | | | | | | | | | | | | | | | | | | | | | | | | |

Student Name: _____ Year: _____

| | 1 | 2 | 3 | 4 | 5 | 6 | 7 | 8 | 9 | 10 | 11 | 12 | 13 | 14 | 15 | 16 | 17 | 18 | 19 | 20 | 21 | 22 | 23 | 24 | 25 | 26 | 27 | 28 | 29 | 30 | 31 |
|---|---|---|---|---|---|---|---|---|---|---|---|---|---|---|---|---|---|---|---|---|---|---|---|---|---|---|---|---|---|---|---|---|
| Sept | | | | | | | | | | | | | | | | | | | | | | | | | | | | | | | |
| Oct | | | | | | | | | | | | | | | | | | | | | | | | | | | | | | | |
| Nov | | | | | | | | | | | | | | | | | | | | | | | | | | | | | | | |
| Dec | | | | | | | | | | | | | | | | | | | | | | | | | | | | | | | |
| Jan | | | | | | | | | | | | | | | | | | | | | | | | | | | | | | | |
| Feb | | | | | | | | | | | | | | | | | | | | | | | | | | | | | | | |
| Mar | | | | | | | | | | | | | | | | | | | | | | | | | | | | | | | |
| Apr | | | | | | | | | | | | | | | | | | | | | | | | | | | | | | | |
| May | | | | | | | | | | | | | | | | | | | | | | | | | | | | | | | |
| Jun | | | | | | | | | | | | | | | | | | | | | | | | | | | | | | | |
| Jul | | | | | | | | | | | | | | | | | | | | | | | | | | | | | | | |
| Aug | | | | | | | | | | | | | | | | | | | | | | | | | | | | | | | |

| | Sept | Oct | Nov | Dec | Jan | Feb | Mar | Apr | May | Jun | Jul | Aug | **Year** |
|---|---|---|---|---|---|---|---|---|---|---|---|---|---|
| E=Excused | | | | | | | | | | | | | |
| T = Tardy | | | | | | | | | | | | | |
| H = Half day | | | | | | | | | | | | | |
| U = Unexcused | | | | | | | | | | | | | |
| P = Present | | | | | | | | | | | | | |

# Personal Data Sheet

If found, Please return to:

Name: _____

Address: _____

City: _____ State: _____ Zip Code: _____

Telephone Number: (_____) _____

Date of Birth: _____ Social Security Number: _____

Place of Birth (City, Country, State, Country): _____

Mother's Maiden Name: _____

Father's Name: _____

**Emergency Contact**

Name: _____

Address: _____

City: _____ State: _____ Zip Code: _____

Telephone Number: (_____) _____

Health Alerts, etc: _____

_____

_____

_____

Medical Insurance: _____

_____

_____

(See Other Side for Medical History)

Summary of Immunization:

| Immunization | Vaccine | | Date (MM/DD/YY) |
|---|---|---|---|
| Diptheria, **T**etanus, **P**ertussis | DTP/Dt/Td | T1 | |
| | DTP/Dt/Td | T2 | |
| DTP/DT/Td | DTP/Dt/Td | T3 | |
| Circle type of Vaccine | DTP/Dt/Td | T4 | |
| | DTP/Dt/Td | T5 | |
| | DTP/Dt/Td | T6 | |
| Polio: | OPV/IPV | P1 | |
| OPV (by mouth) | OPV/IPV | P2 | |
| IPV (injectable) | OPV/IPV | P3 | |
| Circle type of Vaccine | OPV/IPV | P4 | |
| | OPV/IPV | P5 | |
| **Measles** (Ruboella, Red Measles, 10 Day Measles) | Measles | M1 | |
| **Rubella** (German Measles, 3Day Measles) | Rubella | R1 | |
| **Mumps** | Mumps | U1 | |
| **Hib Vaccine** | Hib | H1 | |

Serious Illnesses or accidents: _____

_____

_____

_____

_____

Schools Attended (List dates, addresses, etc.)

_____

_____

_____

_____

_____

100

# Life Goal Planning Sheet

By: _____ Date: _____

---

**Long Term Goals (5-20 years from now)**

Spiritual: _____

_____

_____

Academic: _____

_____

_____

Personal: _____

_____

_____

Financial: _____

_____

_____

Social: _____

_____

_____

Physical: _____

_____

_____

Civic: _____

_____

_____

Other: _____

_____

_____

---

**Intermediate Goals (Two to Five years from now)**

Spiritual: _____

_____

_____

Academic: _____

_____

_____

Personal: _____

_____

_____

Financial: _____

_____

_____

Social: _____

_____

_____

Physical: _____

_____

_____

Civic: _____

_____

_____

Other: _____

_____

_____

# Dates to Remember
## Birthdays and Anniversaries

| January | February | March |
|---|---|---|
| April | May | June |
| July | August | September |
| October | November | December |

## Short Term Goals (6 months-2 years from now)

Spiritual: _____

_____

_____

Academic: _____

_____

_____

Personal: _____

_____

_____

Financial: _____

_____

_____

Social: _____

_____

_____

Physical: _____

_____

_____

Civic: _____

_____

_____

Other: _____

_____

_____

## Immediate Goals (Now to 6 months from now)

Spiritual: _____

_____

_____

Academic: _____

_____

_____

Personal: _____

_____

_____

Financial: _____

_____

_____

Social: _____

_____

_____

Physical: _____

_____

_____

Civic: _____

_____

_____

Other: _____

_____

_____

# Commemorative Days & Holidays

## January

New Year's Day . . . . . . . . . . . . . . . . . . . . . . . . . . . . . . . . January 1st
Martin Luther King, Jr. Day . . . . . . . . . . . . . . . . . . . . . . 3rd Monday in January

## February

Lincoln's Birthday* . . . . . . . . . . . . . . . . . . . . . . . . . . . . . February 12
St. Valentine's Day* . . . . . . . . . . . . . . . . . . . . . . . . . . . . . February 14
Washington's Birthday* . . . . . . . . . . . . . . . . . . . . . . . . . . February 22
President's Day . . . . . . . . . . . . . . . . . . . . . . . . . . 3rd Monday in February

## March

St. Patrick's Day* . . . . . . . . . . . . . . . . . . . . . . . . . . . . . . March 17
Easter 1997 . . . . . . . . . . . . . . . . . . . . . . . . . . . . . . . . . . March 30

## April

Easter Day — 1994 . . . . . . . . . . . . . . . . . . . . . . . . . . . . . . April 3
1995 . . . . . . . . . . . . . . . . . . . . . . . . . . . . . . . . . . . . . . . April 16
1996 . . . . . . . . . . . . . . . . . . . . . . . . . . . . . . . . . . . . . . . April 7
1997 . . . . . . . . . . . . . . . . . . . . . . . . . . . . . . . . . . . . . . . March 30
1998 . . . . . . . . . . . . . . . . . . . . . . . . . . . . . . . . . . . . . . . April 12

## May

Mother's Day* . . . . . . . . . . . . . . . . . . . . . . . . . . . . . . 2nd Sunday in May
Memorial Day . . . . . . . . . . . . . . . . . . . . . . . . . . . . . Last Monday in May

## June

Flag Day* . . . . . . . . . . . . . . . . . . . . . . . . . . . . . . . . . . . . June 14
Father's Day* . . . . . . . . . . . . . . . . . . . . . . . . . . . . . . 3rd Sunday in June

## July

Independence Day . . . . . . . . . . . . . . . . . . . . . . . . . . . . . . . . July 4

## September

Labor Day . . . . . . . . . . . . . . . . . . . . . . . . . . . . 1st Monday in September
Grandparent's Day* . . . . . . . . . . . . . . . . . . . . . . 2nd Sunday in September

## October

Columbus Day . . . . . . . . . . . . . . . . . . . . . . . . . Oct 12/2nd Monday in Oct
Halloween* . . . . . . . . . . . . . . . . . . . . . . . . . . . . . . . . . October 31
All Saints Day* . . . . . . . . . . . . . . . . . . . . . . . . . . . . . . November 1

## November

Election Day* . . . . . . . . . . . . . . . . . . . . . . . . . . . 1st Tuesday in November
Veteran's Day . . . . . . . . . . . . . . . . . . . . . . . . . . . . . . November 11
Thanksgiving Day . . . . . . . . . . . . . . . . . . . . . . . 4th Thursday in November

## December

Christmas Day . . . . . . . . . . . . . . . . . . . . . . . . . . . . . . . December 25

* Not a legal holiday.
Note: When a legal holiday falls on a Saturday or Sunday, the holiday is usually observed by banks, government offices and buildings, and schools on the Friday before the holiday or the Monday after the holiday.

# 1996-1997 Planning Sheet

## 1996

| January | February | March |
|---|---|---|
| 1 2 3 4 5 6 | 1 2 3 | 1 2 |
| 7 8 9 10 11 12 13 | 4 5 6 7 8 9 10 | 3 4 5 6 7 8 9 |
| 14 15 16 17 18 19 20 | 11 12 13 14 15 16 17 | 10 11 12 13 14 15 16 |
| 21 22 23 24 25 26 27 | 18 19 20 21 22 23 24 | 17 18 19 20 21 22 23 |
| 28 29 30 31 | 25 26 27 28 29 | 24 25 26 27 28 29 30 |
| | | 31 |

| April | May | June |
|---|---|---|
| 1 2 3 4 5 6 | 1 2 3 4 | 1 |
| 7 8 9 10 11 12 13 | 5 6 7 8 9 10 11 | 2 3 4 5 6 7 8 |
| 14 15 16 17 18 19 20 | 12 13 14 15 16 17 18 | 9 10 11 12 13 14 15 |
| 21 22 23 24 25 26 27 | 19 20 21 22 23 24 25 | 16 17 18 19 20 21 22 |
| 28 29 30 | 26 27 28 29 30 31 | 23 24 25 26 27 28 29 |
| | | 30 |

| July | August | September |
|---|---|---|
| 1 2 3 4 5 6 | 1 2 3 | 1 2 3 4 5 6 7 |
| 7 8 9 10 11 12 13 | 4 5 6 7 8 9 10 | 8 9 10 11 12 13 14 |
| 14 15 16 17 18 19 20 | 11 12 13 14 15 16 17 | 15 16 17 18 19 20 21 |
| 21 22 23 24 25 26 27 | 18 19 20 21 22 23 24 | 22 23 24 25 26 27 28 |
| 28 29 30 31 | 25 26 27 28 29 30 31 | 29 30 |

| October | November | December |
|---|---|---|
| 1 2 3 4 5 | 1 2 | 1 2 3 4 5 6 7 |
| 6 7 8 9 10 11 12 | 3 4 5 6 7 8 9 | 8 9 10 11 12 13 14 |
| 13 14 15 16 17 18 19 | 10 11 12 13 14 15 16 | 15 16 17 18 19 20 21 |
| 20 21 22 23 24 25 26 | 17 18 19 20 21 22 23 | 22 23 24 25 26 27 28 |
| 27 28 29 30 31 | 24 25 26 27 28 29 30 | 29 30 31 |

## 1997

| January | February | March |
|---|---|---|
| 1 2 3 4 | 1 | 1 |
| 5 6 7 8 9 10 11 | 2 3 4 5 6 7 8 | 2 3 4 5 6 7 8 |
| 12 13 14 15 16 17 18 | 9 10 11 12 13 14 15 | 9 10 11 12 13 14 15 |
| 19 20 21 22 23 24 25 | 16 17 18 19 20 21 22 | 16 17 18 19 20 21 22 |
| 26 27 28 29 30 31 | 23 24 25 26 27 28 | 23 24 25 26 27 28 29 |
| | | 30 31 |

| April | May | June |
|---|---|---|
| 1 2 3 4 5 | 1 2 3 | 1 2 3 4 5 6 7 |
| 6 7 8 9 10 11 12 | 4 5 6 7 8 9 10 | 8 9 10 11 12 13 14 |
| 13 14 15 16 17 18 19 | 11 12 13 14 15 16 17 | 15 16 17 18 19 20 21 |
| 20 21 22 23 24 25 26 | 18 19 20 21 22 23 24 | 22 23 24 25 26 27 28 |
| 27 28 29 30 | 25 26 27 28 29 30 31 | 29 30 |
| | 30 31 | |

| July | August | September |
|---|---|---|
| 1 2 3 4 5 | 1 2 | 1 2 3 4 5 6 |
| 6 7 8 9 10 11 12 | 3 4 5 6 7 8 9 | 7 8 9 10 11 12 13 |
| 13 14 15 16 17 18 19 | 10 11 12 13 14 15 16 | 14 15 16 17 18 19 20 |
| 20 21 22 23 24 25 26 | 17 18 19 20 21 22 23 | 21 22 23 24 25 26 27 |
| 27 28 29 30 31 | 24 25 26 27 28 29 30 | 28 29 30 30 |
| | 31 | |

| October | November | December |
|---|---|---|
| 1 2 3 4 | 1 | 1 2 3 4 5 6 |
| 5 6 7 8 9 10 11 | 2 3 4 5 6 7 8 | 7 8 9 10 11 12 13 |
| 12 13 14 15 16 17 18 | 9 10 11 12 13 14 15 | 14 15 16 17 18 19 20 |
| 19 20 21 22 23 24 25 | 16 17 18 19 20 21 22 | 21 22 23 24 25 26 27 |
| 26 27 28 29 30 31 | 23 24 25 26 27 28 29 | 28 29 30 31 |
| | 30 | |

*Dates to Remember*

# Goals For 1996-1997

Academic:

Personal:

Spiritual:

Social:

Physical:

Civic:

# 1997-1998 Planning Sheet

## 1997

| January | | | | | | |
|---|---|---|---|---|---|---|
| | | 1 | 2 | 3 | 4 | |
| 5 | 6 | 7 | 8 | 9 | 10 | 11 |
| 12 | 13 | 14 | 15 | 16 | 17 | 18 |
| 19 | 20 | 21 | 22 | 23 | 24 | 25 |
| 26 | 27 | 28 | 29 | 30 | 31 | |

| February | | | | | | |
|---|---|---|---|---|---|---|
| | | | | | | 1 |
| 2 | 3 | 4 | 5 | 6 | 7 | 8 |
| 9 | 10 | 11 | 12 | 13 | 14 | 15 |
| 16 | 17 | 18 | 19 | 20 | 21 | 22 |
| 23 | 24 | 25 | 26 | 27 | 28 | |

| March | | | | | | |
|---|---|---|---|---|---|---|
| | | | | | | 1 |
| 2 | 3 | 4 | 5 | 6 | 7 | 8 |
| 9 | 10 | 11 | 12 | 13 | 14 | 15 |
| 16 | 17 | 18 | 19 | 20 | 21 | 22 |
| 23 | 24 | 25 | 26 | 27 | 28 | 29 |
| 30 | 31 | | | | | |

| April | | | | | | |
|---|---|---|---|---|---|---|
| | | 1 | 2 | 3 | 4 | 5 |
| 6 | 7 | 8 | 9 | 10 | 11 | 12 |
| 13 | 14 | 15 | 16 | 17 | 18 | 19 |
| 20 | 21 | 22 | 23 | 24 | 25 | 26 |
| 27 | 28 | 29 | 30 | | | |

| May | | | | | | |
|---|---|---|---|---|---|---|
| | | | | 1 | 2 | 3 |
| 4 | 5 | 6 | 7 | 8 | 9 | 10 |
| 11 | 12 | 13 | 14 | 15 | 16 | 17 |
| 18 | 19 | 20 | 21 | 22 | 23 | 24 |
| 25 | 26 | 27 | 28 | 29 | 30 | 31 |
| 30 | 31 | | | | | |

| June | | | | | | |
|---|---|---|---|---|---|---|
| 1 | 2 | 3 | 4 | 5 | 6 | 7 |
| 8 | 9 | 10 | 11 | 12 | 13 | 14 |
| 15 | 16 | 17 | 18 | 19 | 20 | 21 |
| 22 | 23 | 24 | 25 | 26 | 27 | 28 |
| 29 | 30 | | | | | |

| July | | | | | | |
|---|---|---|---|---|---|---|
| | | 1 | 2 | 3 | 4 | 5 |
| 6 | 7 | 8 | 9 | 10 | 11 | 12 |
| 13 | 14 | 15 | 16 | 17 | 18 | 19 |
| 20 | 21 | 22 | 23 | 24 | 25 | 26 |
| 27 | 28 | 29 | 30 | 31 | | |

| August | | | | | | |
|---|---|---|---|---|---|---|
| | | | | | 1 | 2 |
| 3 | 4 | 5 | 6 | 7 | 8 | 9 |
| 10 | 11 | 12 | 13 | 14 | 15 | 16 |
| 17 | 18 | 19 | 20 | 21 | 22 | 23 |
| 24 | 25 | 26 | 27 | 28 | 29 | 30 |
| 31 | | | | | | |

| September | | | | | | |
|---|---|---|---|---|---|---|
| | 1 | 2 | 3 | 4 | 5 | 6 |
| 7 | 8 | 9 | 10 | 11 | 12 | 13 |
| 14 | 15 | 16 | 17 | 18 | 19 | 20 |
| 21 | 22 | 23 | 24 | 25 | 26 | 27 |
| 28 | 29 | 30 | 30 | | | |

| October | | | | | | |
|---|---|---|---|---|---|---|
| | | 1 | 2 | 3 | 4 | |
| 5 | 6 | 7 | 8 | 9 | 10 | 11 |
| 12 | 13 | 14 | 15 | 16 | 17 | 18 |
| 19 | 20 | 21 | 22 | 23 | 24 | 25 |
| 26 | 27 | 28 | 29 | 30 | 31 | |

| November | | | | | | |
|---|---|---|---|---|---|---|
| | | | | | | 1 |
| 2 | 3 | 4 | 5 | 6 | 7 | 8 |
| 9 | 10 | 11 | 12 | 13 | 14 | 15 |
| 16 | 17 | 18 | 19 | 20 | 21 | 22 |
| 23 | 24 | 25 | 26 | 27 | 28 | 29 |
| 30 | | | | | | |

| December | | | | | | |
|---|---|---|---|---|---|---|
| | 1 | 2 | 3 | 4 | 5 | 6 |
| 7 | 8 | 9 | 10 | 11 | 12 | 13 |
| 14 | 15 | 16 | 17 | 18 | 19 | 20 |
| 21 | 22 | 23 | 24 | 25 | 26 | 27 |
| 28 | 29 | 30 | 31 | | | |

## 1998

| January | | | | | | |
|---|---|---|---|---|---|---|
| | | | 1 | 2 | 3 | |
| 4 | 5 | 6 | 7 | 8 | 9 | 10 |
| 11 | 12 | 13 | 14 | 15 | 16 | 17 |
| 18 | 19 | 20 | 21 | 22 | 23 | 24 |
| 25 | 26 | 27 | 28 | 29 | 30 | 31 |

| February | | | | | | |
|---|---|---|---|---|---|---|
| 1 | 2 | 3 | 4 | 5 | 6 | 7 |
| 8 | 9 | 10 | 11 | 12 | 13 | 14 |
| 15 | 16 | 17 | 18 | 19 | 20 | 21 |
| 22 | 23 | 24 | 25 | 26 | 27 | 28 |

| March | | | | | | |
|---|---|---|---|---|---|---|
| 1 | 2 | 3 | 4 | 5 | 6 | 7 |
| 8 | 9 | 10 | 11 | 12 | 13 | 14 |
| 15 | 16 | 17 | 18 | 19 | 20 | 21 |
| 22 | 23 | 24 | 25 | 26 | 27 | 28 |
| 29 | 30 | 31 | | | | |

| April | | | | | | |
|---|---|---|---|---|---|---|
| | | 1 | 2 | 3 | 4 | |
| 5 | 6 | 7 | 8 | 9 | 10 | 11 |
| 12 | 13 | 14 | 15 | 16 | 17 | 18 |
| 19 | 20 | 21 | 22 | 23 | 24 | 25 |
| 26 | 27 | 28 | 29 | 30 | | |

| May | | | | | | |
|---|---|---|---|---|---|---|
| | | | | | 1 | 2 |
| 3 | 4 | 5 | 6 | 7 | 8 | 9 |
| 10 | 11 | 12 | 13 | 14 | 15 | 16 |
| 17 | 18 | 19 | 20 | 21 | 22 | 23 |
| 24 | 25 | 26 | 27 | 28 | 29 | 30 |
| 31 | | | | | | |

| June | | | | | | |
|---|---|---|---|---|---|---|
| | 1 | 2 | 3 | 4 | 5 | 6 |
| 7 | 8 | 9 | 10 | 11 | 12 | 13 |
| 14 | 15 | 16 | 17 | 18 | 19 | 20 |
| 21 | 22 | 23 | 24 | 25 | 26 | 27 |
| 28 | 29 | 30 | | | | |

| July | | | | | | |
|---|---|---|---|---|---|---|
| | | 1 | 2 | 3 | 4 | |
| 5 | 6 | 7 | 8 | 9 | 10 | 11 |
| 12 | 13 | 14 | 15 | 16 | 17 | 18 |
| 19 | 20 | 21 | 22 | 23 | 24 | 25 |
| 26 | 27 | 28 | 29 | 30 | 31 | |

| August | | | | | | |
|---|---|---|---|---|---|---|
| | | | | | | 1 |
| 2 | 3 | 4 | 5 | 6 | 7 | 8 |
| 9 | 10 | 11 | 12 | 13 | 14 | 15 |
| 16 | 17 | 18 | 19 | 20 | 21 | 22 |
| 23 | 24 | 25 | 26 | 27 | 28 | 29 |
| 30 | 31 | | | | | |

| September | | | | | | |
|---|---|---|---|---|---|---|
| | | 1 | 2 | 3 | 4 | 5 |
| 6 | 7 | 8 | 9 | 10 | 11 | 12 |
| 13 | 14 | 15 | 16 | 17 | 18 | 19 |
| 20 | 21 | 22 | 23 | 24 | 25 | 26 |
| 27 | 28 | 29 | 30 | | | |

| October | | | | | | |
|---|---|---|---|---|---|---|
| | | | 1 | 2 | 3 | |
| 4 | 5 | 6 | 7 | 8 | 0 | 10 |
| 11 | 12 | 13 | 14 | 15 | 16 | 17 |
| 18 | 19 | 20 | 21 | 22 | 23 | 24 |
| 25 | 26 | 27 | 28 | 29 | 30 | 31 |

| November | | | | | | |
|---|---|---|---|---|---|---|
| 1 | 2 | 3 | 4 | 5 | 6 | 7 |
| 8 | 9 | 10 | 11 | 12 | 13 | 14 |
| 15 | 16 | 17 | 18 | 19 | 20 | 21 |
| 22 | 23 | 24 | 25 | 26 | 27 | 28 |
| 29 | 30 | | | | | |

| December | | | | | | |
|---|---|---|---|---|---|---|
| | 1 | 2 | 3 | 4 | 5 | |
| 6 | 7 | 8 | 9 | 10 | 11 | 12 |
| 13 | 14 | 15 | 16 | 17 | 18 | 19 |
| 20 | 21 | 22 | 23 | 24 | 25 | 26 |
| 27 | 28 | 29 | 30 | 31 | | |

*Dates to Remember*

# Goals For 1997-1998

**Academic:**

**Personal:**

**Spiritual:**

**Social:**

**Physical:**

**Civic:**

# 1998-1999 Planning Sheet

## 1998

### January
|   |   |   | 1 | 2 | 3 |
| 4 | 5 | 6 | 7 | 8 | 9 | 10 |
| 11 | 12 | 13 | 14 | 15 | 16 | 17 |
| 18 | 19 | 20 | 21 | 22 | 23 | 24 |
| 25 | 26 | 27 | 28 | 29 | 30 | 31 |

### February
| 1 | 2 | 3 | 4 | 5 | 6 | 7 |
| 8 | 9 | 10 | 11 | 12 | 13 | 14 |
| 15 | 16 | 17 | 18 | 19 | 20 | 21 |
| 22 | 23 | 24 | 25 | 26 | 27 | 28 |

### March
| 1 | 2 | 3 | 4 | 5 | 6 | 7 |
| 8 | 9 | 10 | 11 | 12 | 13 | 14 |
| 15 | 16 | 17 | 18 | 19 | 20 | 21 |
| 22 | 23 | 24 | 25 | 26 | 27 | 28 |
| 29 | 30 | 31 |

### April
|   |   |   | 1 | 2 | 3 | 4 |
| 5 | 6 | 7 | 8 | 9 | 10 | 11 |
| 12 | 13 | 14 | 15 | 16 | 17 | 18 |
| 19 | 20 | 21 | 22 | 23 | 24 | 25 |
| 26 | 27 | 28 | 29 | 30 |

### May
|   |   |   |   |   | 1 | 2 |
| 3 | 4 | 5 | 6 | 7 | 8 | 9 |
| 10 | 11 | 12 | 13 | 14 | 15 | 16 |
| 17 | 18 | 19 | 20 | 21 | 22 | 23 |
| 24 | 25 | 26 | 27 | 28 | 29 | 30 |
| 31 |

### June
|   | 1 | 2 | 3 | 4 | 5 | 6 |
| 7 | 8 | 9 | 10 | 11 | 12 | 13 |
| 14 | 15 | 16 | 17 | 18 | 19 | 20 |
| 21 | 22 | 23 | 24 | 25 | 26 | 27 |
| 28 | 29 | 30 |

### July
|   |   |   | 1 | 2 | 3 | 4 |
| 5 | 6 | 7 | 8 | 9 | 10 | 11 |
| 12 | 13 | 14 | 15 | 16 | 17 | 18 |
| 19 | 20 | 21 | 22 | 23 | 24 | 25 |
| 26 | 27 | 28 | 29 | 30 | 31 |

### August
|   |   |   |   |   |   | 1 |
| 2 | 3 | 4 | 5 | 6 | 7 | 8 |
| 9 | 10 | 11 | 12 | 13 | 14 | 15 |
| 16 | 17 | 18 | 19 | 20 | 21 | 22 |
| 23 | 24 | 25 | 26 | 27 | 28 | 29 |
| 30 | 31 |

### September
|   |   | 1 | 2 | 3 | 4 | 5 |
| 6 | 7 | 8 | 9 | 10 | 11 | 12 |
| 13 | 14 | 15 | 16 | 17 | 18 | 19 |
| 20 | 21 | 22 | 23 | 24 | 25 | 26 |
| 27 | 28 | 29 | 30 |

### October
|   |   |   | 1 | 2 | 3 |
| 4 | 5 | 6 | 7 | 8 | 0 | 10 |
| 11 | 12 | 13 | 14 | 15 | 16 | 17 |
| 18 | 19 | 20 | 21 | 22 | 23 | 24 |
| 25 | 26 | 27 | 28 | 29 | 30 | 31 |

### November
| 1 | 2 | 3 | 4 | 5 | 6 | 7 |
| 8 | 9 | 10 | 11 | 12 | 13 | 14 |
| 15 | 16 | 17 | 18 | 19 | 20 | 21 |
| 22 | 23 | 24 | 25 | 26 | 27 | 28 |
| 29 | 30 |

### December
|   | 1 | 2 | 3 | 4 | 5 |
| 6 | 7 | 8 | 9 | 10 | 11 | 12 |
| 13 | 14 | 15 | 16 | 17 | 18 | 19 |
| 20 | 21 | 22 | 23 | 24 | 25 | 26 |
| 27 | 28 | 29 | 30 | 31 |

## 1999

### January
|   |   |   |   |   | 1 | 2 |
| 3 | 4 | 5 | 6 | 7 | 8 | 9 |
| 10 | 11 | 12 | 13 | 14 | 15 | 16 |
| 17 | 18 | 19 | 20 | 21 | 22 | 23 |
| 24 | 25 | 26 | 27 | 28 | 29 | 30 |
| 31 |

### February
|   | 1 | 2 | 3 | 4 | 5 | 6 |
| 7 | 8 | 9 | 10 | 11 | 12 | 13 |
| 14 | 15 | 16 | 17 | 18 | 19 | 20 |
| 21 | 22 | 23 | 24 | 25 | 26 | 27 |
| 28 |

### March
|   | 1 | 2 | 3 | 4 | 5 | 6 |
| 7 | 8 | 9 | 10 | 11 | 12 | 13 |
| 14 | 15 | 16 | 17 | 18 | 19 | 20 |
| 21 | 22 | 23 | 24 | 25 | 26 | 27 |
| 28 | 29 | 30 | 31 |

### April
|   |   |   | 1 | 2 | 3 |
| 4 | 5 | 6 | 7 | 8 | 9 | 10 |
| 11 | 12 | 13 | 14 | 15 | 16 | 17 |
| 18 | 19 | 20 | 21 | 22 | 23 | 24 |
| 25 | 26 | 27 | 28 | 29 | 30 |

### May
|   |   |   |   |   |   | 1 |
| 2 | 3 | 4 | 5 | 6 | 7 | 8 |
| 9 | 10 | 11 | 12 | 13 | 14 | 15 |
| 16 | 17 | 18 | 19 | 20 | 21 | 22 |
| 23 | 24 | 25 | 26 | 27 | 28 | 29 |
| 30 | 31 |

### June
|   |   | 1 | 2 | 3 | 4 | 5 |
| 6 | 7 | 8 | 9 | 10 | 11 | 12 |
| 13 | 14 | 15 | 16 | 17 | 18 | 19 |
| 20 | 21 | 22 | 23 | 24 | 25 | 26 |
| 27 | 28 | 29 | 30 |

### July
|   |   |   |   | 1 | 2 | 3 |
| 4 | 5 | 6 | 7 | 8 | 9 | 10 |
| 11 | 12 | 13 | 14 | 15 | 16 | 17 |
| 18 | 19 | 20 | 21 | 22 | 23 | 24 |
| 25 | 26 | 27 | 28 | 29 | 30 | 31 |

### August
| 1 | 2 | 3 | 4 | 5 | 6 | 7 |
| 8 | 9 | 10 | 11 | 12 | 13 | 14 |
| 15 | 16 | 17 | 18 | 19 | 20 | 21 |
| 22 | 23 | 24 | 25 | 26 | 27 | 28 |
| 29 | 30 | 31 |

### September
|   |   |   | 1 | 2 | 3 | 4 |
| 5 | 6 | 7 | 8 | 9 | 10 | 11 |
| 12 | 13 | 14 | 15 | 16 | 17 | 18 |
| 19 | 20 | 21 | 22 | 23 | 24 | 25 |
| 26 | 27 | 28 | 29 | 30 |

### October
|   |   |   |   |   | 1 | 2 |
| 3 | 4 | 5 | 6 | 7 | 8 | 9 |
| 10 | 11 | 12 | 13 | 14 | 15 | 16 |
| 17 | 18 | 19 | 20 | 21 | 22 | 23 |
| 24 | 25 | 26 | 27 | 28 | 29 | 30 |
| 31 |

### November
|   | 1 | 2 | 3 | 4 | 5 | 6 |
| 7 | 8 | 9 | 10 | 11 | 12 | 13 |
| 14 | 15 | 16 | 17 | 18 | 19 | 20 |
| 21 | 22 | 23 | 24 | 25 | 26 | 27 |
| 28 | 29 | 30 |

### December
|   |   |   | 1 | 2 | 3 | 4 |
| 5 | 6 | 7 | 8 | 9 | 10 | 11 |
| 12 | 13 | 14 | 15 | 16 | 17 | 18 |
| 19 | 20 | 21 | 22 | 23 | 24 | 25 |
| 26 | 27 | 28 | 29 | 30 | 31 |

*Dates to Remember*

# Goals For 1998-1999

**Academic:**

**Personal:**

**Spiritual:**

**Social:**

**Physical:**

**Civic:**

# 1999-2000 Planning Sheet

## 1999

| January | February | March |
|---|---|---|
| 1 2 | 1 2 3 4 5 6 | 1 2 3 4 5 6 |
| 3 4 5 6 7 8 9 | 7 8 9 10 11 12 13 | 7 8 9 10 11 12 13 |
| 10 11 12 13 14 15 16 | 14 15 16 17 18 19 20 | 14 15 16 17 18 19 20 |
| 17 18 19 20 21 22 23 | 21 22 23 24 25 26 27 | 21 22 23 24 25 26 27 |
| 24 25 26 27 28 29 30 | 28 | 28 29 30 31 |
| 31 | | |

| April | May | June |
|---|---|---|
| 1 2 3 | 1 | 1 2 3 4 5 |
| 4 5 6 7 8 9 10 | 2 3 4 5 6 7 8 | 6 7 8 9 10 11 12 |
| 11 12 13 14 15 16 17 | 9 10 11 12 13 14 15 | 13 14 15 16 17 18 19 |
| 18 19 20 21 22 23 24 | 16 17 18 19 20 21 22 | 20 21 22 23 24 25 26 |
| 25 26 27 28 29 30 | 23 24 25 26 27 28 29 | 27 28 29 30 |
| | 30 31 | |

| July | August | September |
|---|---|---|
| 1 2 3 | 1 2 3 4 5 6 7 | 1 2 3 4 |
| 4 5 6 7 8 9 10 | 8 9 10 11 12 13 14 | 5 6 7 8 9 10 11 |
| 11 12 13 14 15 16 17 | 15 16 17 18 19 20 21 | 12 13 14 15 16 17 18 |
| 18 19 20 21 22 23 24 | 22 23 24 25 26 27 28 | 19 20 21 22 23 24 25 |
| 25 26 27 28 29 30 31 | 29 30 31 | 26 27 28 29 30 |

| October | November | December |
|---|---|---|
| 1 2 | 1 2 3 4 5 6 | 1 2 3 4 |
| 3 4 5 6 7 8 9 | 7 8 9 10 11 12 13 | 5 6 7 8 9 10 11 |
| 10 11 12 13 14 15 16 | 14 15 16 17 18 19 20 | 12 13 14 15 16 17 18 |
| 17 18 19 20 21 22 23 | 21 22 23 24 25 26 27 | 19 20 21 22 23 24 25 |
| 24 25 26 27 28 29 30 | 28 29 30 | 26 27 28 29 30 31 |
| 31 | | |

## 2000

| January | February | March |
|---|---|---|
| 1 | 1 2 3 4 5 | 1 2 3 4 |
| 2 3 4 5 6 7 8 | 6 7 8 9 10 11 12 | 5 6 7 8 9 10 11 |
| 9 10 11 12 13 14 15 | 13 14 15 16 17 18 19 | 12 13 14 15 16 17 18 |
| 16 17 | 20 21 22 23 24 25 26 | 19 20 21 22 23 24 25 |
| 30 31 | 27 28 29 | 26 27 28 29 30 31 |

| April | May | June |
|---|---|---|
| 1 | 1 2 3 4 5 6 | 1 2 3 |
| 2 3 4 5 6 7 8 | 7 8 9 10 11 12 13 | 4 5 6 7 8 9 10 |
| 9 10 11 12 13 14 15 | 14 15 16 17 18 19 20 | 11 12 13 14 15 16 17 |
| 16 17 18 19 20 21 22 | 21 22 23 24 25 26 27 | 18 19 20 21 22 23 24 |
| 23 24 25 26 27 28 29 | 28 29 30 31 | 25 26 27 28 29 30 |
| 30 | | |

| July | August | September |
|---|---|---|
| 1 | 1 2 3 4 5 | 1 2 |
| 2 3 4 5 6 7 8 | 6 7 8 9 10 11 12 | 3 4 5 6 7 8 9 |
| 9 10 11 12 13 14 15 | 13 14 15 16 17 18 19 | 10 11 12 13 14 15 16 |
| 16 17 18 19 20 21 22 | 20 21 22 23 24 25 26 | 17 18 19 20 21 22 23 |
| 23 24 25 26 27 28 29 | 27 28 29 30 31 | 24 25 26 27 28 29 30 |
| 30 31 | | |

| October | November | December |
|---|---|---|
| 1 2 3 4 5 6 7 | 1 2 3 4 | 1 2 |
| 8 9 10 11 12 13 14 | 5 6 7 8 9 10 11 | 3 4 5 6 7 8 9 |
| 15 16 17 18 19 20 21 | 12 13 14 15 16 17 18 | 10 11 12 13 14 15 16 |
| 22 23 24 25 26 27 28 | 19 20 21 22 23 24 25 | 17 18 19 20 21 22 23 |
| 29 30 31 | 26 27 28 29 30 | 24 25 26 27 28 29 30 |
| | | 31 |

*Dates to Remember*

# Goals For 1999-2000

Academic:

Personal:

Spiritual:

Social:

Physical:

Civic:

# 2000-2001 Planning Sheet

## 2000

| January | | | | | | |
|---|---|---|---|---|---|---|
| | | | | | | 1 |
| 2 | 3 | 4 | 5 | 6 | 7 | 8 |
| 9 | 10 | 11 | 12 | 13 | 14 | 15 |
| 10 | 11 | 12 | 14 | 15 | 16 | 17 |
| 30 | 31 | | | | | |

| February | | | | | | |
|---|---|---|---|---|---|---|
| | 1 | 2 | 3 | 4 | 5 | |
| 6 | 7 | 8 | 9 | 10 | 11 | 12 |
| 13 | 14 | 15 | 16 | 17 | 18 | 19 |
| 20 | 21 | 22 | 23 | 24 | 25 | 26 |
| 27 | 28 | 29 | | | | |

| March | | | | | | |
|---|---|---|---|---|---|---|
| | | | 1 | 2 | 3 | 4 |
| 5 | 6 | 7 | 8 | 9 | 10 | 11 |
| 12 | 13 | 14 | 15 | 16 | 17 | 18 |
| 19 | 20 | 21 | 22 | 23 | 24 | 25 |
| 26 | 27 | 28 | 29 | 30 | 31 | |

| April | | | | | | |
|---|---|---|---|---|---|---|
| | | | | | | 1 |
| 2 | 3 | 4 | 5 | 6 | 7 | 8 |
| 9 | 10 | 11 | 12 | 13 | 14 | 15 |
| 16 | 17 | 18 | 19 | 20 | 21 | 22 |
| 23 | 24 | 25 | 26 | 27 | 28 | 29 |
| 30 | | | | | | |

| May | | | | | | |
|---|---|---|---|---|---|---|
| | 1 | 2 | 3 | 4 | 5 | 6 |
| 7 | 8 | 9 | 10 | 11 | 12 | 13 |
| 14 | 15 | 16 | 17 | 18 | 19 | 20 |
| 21 | 22 | 23 | 24 | 25 | 26 | 27 |
| 28 | 29 | 30 | 31 | | | |

| June | | | | | | |
|---|---|---|---|---|---|---|
| | | | | 1 | 2 | 3 |
| 4 | 5 | 6 | 7 | 8 | 9 | 10 |
| 11 | 12 | 13 | 14 | 15 | 16 | 17 |
| 18 | 19 | 20 | 21 | 22 | 23 | 24 |
| 25 | 26 | 27 | 28 | 29 | 30 | |

| July | | | | | | |
|---|---|---|---|---|---|---|
| | | | | | | 1 |
| 2 | 3 | 4 | 5 | 6 | 7 | 8 |
| 9 | 10 | 11 | 12 | 13 | 14 | 15 |
| 16 | 17 | 18 | 19 | 20 | 21 | 22 |
| 23 | 24 | 25 | 26 | 27 | 28 | 29 |
| 30 | 31 | | | | | |

| August | | | | | | |
|---|---|---|---|---|---|---|
| | 1 | 2 | 3 | 4 | 5 | |
| 6 | 7 | 8 | 9 | 10 | 11 | 12 |
| 13 | 14 | 15 | 16 | 17 | 18 | 19 |
| 20 | 21 | 22 | 23 | 24 | 25 | 26 |
| 27 | 28 | 29 | 30 | 31 | | |

| September | | | | | | |
|---|---|---|---|---|---|---|
| | | | | | 1 | 2 |
| 3 | 4 | 5 | 6 | 7 | 8 | 9 |
| 10 | 11 | 12 | 13 | 14 | 15 | 16 |
| 17 | 18 | 19 | 20 | 21 | 22 | 23 |
| 24 | 25 | 26 | 27 | 28 | 29 | 30 |

| October | | | | | | |
|---|---|---|---|---|---|---|
| 1 | 2 | 3 | 4 | 5 | 6 | 7 |
| 8 | 9 | 10 | 11 | 12 | 13 | 14 |
| 15 | 16 | 17 | 18 | 19 | 20 | 21 |
| 22 | 23 | 24 | 25 | 26 | 27 | 28 |
| 29 | 30 | 31 | | | | |

| November | | | | | | |
|---|---|---|---|---|---|---|
| | | | 1 | 2 | 3 | 4 |
| 5 | 6 | 7 | 8 | 9 | 10 | 11 |
| 12 | 13 | 14 | 15 | 16 | 17 | 18 |
| 19 | 20 | 21 | 22 | 23 | 24 | 25 |
| 26 | 27 | 28 | 29 | 30 | | |

| December | | | | | | |
|---|---|---|---|---|---|---|
| | | | | | 1 | 2 |
| 3 | 4 | 5 | 6 | 7 | 8 | 9 |
| 10 | 11 | 12 | 13 | 14 | 15 | 16 |
| 17 | 18 | 19 | 20 | 21 | 22 | 23 |
| 24 | 25 | 26 | 27 | 28 | 29 | 30 |
| 31 | | | | | | |

## 2001

| January | | | | | | |
|---|---|---|---|---|---|---|
| 1 | 2 | 3 | 4 | 5 | 6 | |
| 7 | 8 | 9 | 10 | 11 | 12 | 13 |
| 14 | 15 | 16 | 17 | 18 | 19 | 20 |
| 21 | 22 | 23 | 24 | 25 | 26 | 27 |
| 28 | 29 | 30 | 31 | | | |

| February | | | | | | |
|---|---|---|---|---|---|---|
| | | | 1 | 2 | 3 | |
| 4 | 5 | 6 | 7 | 8 | 9 | 10 |
| 11 | 12 | 13 | 14 | 15 | 16 | 17 |
| 18 | 29 | 20 | 21 | 22 | 23 | 24 |
| 25 | 26 | 27 | 28 | 29 | | |

| March | | | | | | |
|---|---|---|---|---|---|---|
| | | | 1 | 2 | 3 | |
| 4 | 5 | 6 | 7 | 8 | 9 | 10 |
| 11 | 12 | 13 | 14 | 15 | 16 | 17 |
| 18 | 19 | 20 | 21 | 22 | 23 | 24 |
| 25 | 26 | 27 | 28 | 29 | 30 | 31 |

| April | | | | | | |
|---|---|---|---|---|---|---|
| 1 | 2 | 3 | 4 | 5 | 6 | 7 |
| 8 | 9 | 10 | 11 | 12 | 13 | 14 |
| 15 | 16 | 17 | 18 | 19 | 20 | 21 |
| 22 | 23 | 24 | 25 | 26 | 27 | 28 |
| 29 | 30 | | | | | |

| May | | | | | | |
|---|---|---|---|---|---|---|
| | 1 | 2 | 3 | 4 | 5 | |
| 6 | 7 | 8 | 9 | 10 | 11 | 12 |
| 13 | 14 | 15 | 16 | 17 | 18 | 19 |
| 20 | 21 | 22 | 23 | 24 | 25 | 26 |
| 27 | 28 | 29 | 30 | 31 | | |

| June | | | | | | |
|---|---|---|---|---|---|---|
| | | | | | 1 | 2 |
| 3 | 4 | 5 | 6 | 7 | 8 | 9 |
| 10 | 11 | 12 | 13 | 14 | 15 | 16 |
| 17 | 18 | 19 | 20 | 21 | 22 | 23 |
| 24 | 25 | 26 | 27 | 38 | 29 | 30 |

| July | | | | | | |
|---|---|---|---|---|---|---|
| 1 | 2 | 3 | 4 | 5 | 6 | 7 |
| 8 | 9 | 10 | 11 | 12 | 13 | 14 |
| 15 | 16 | 17 | 18 | 19 | 20 | 21 |
| 22 | 23 | 24 | 25 | 26 | 27 | 28 |
| 29 | 30 | 31 | | | | |

| August | | | | | | |
|---|---|---|---|---|---|---|
| | | 1 | 2 | 3 | 4 | |
| 5 | 6 | 7 | 8 | 9 | 10 | 11 |
| 12 | 13 | 14 | 15 | 16 | 17 | 18 |
| 19 | 20 | 21 | 22 | 23 | 24 | 25 |
| 26 | 27 | 28 | 29 | 30 | 31 | |

| September | | | | | | |
|---|---|---|---|---|---|---|
| | | | | | | 1 |
| 2 | 3 | 4 | 5 | 6 | 7 | 8 |
| 9 | 10 | 11 | 12 | 13 | 14 | 15 |
| 16 | 17 | 18 | 19 | 20 | 21 | 22 |
| 23 | 24 | 25 | 26 | 27 | 28 | 29 |
| 30 | | | | | | |

| October | | | | | | |
|---|---|---|---|---|---|---|
| | 1 | 2 | 3 | 4 | 5 | 6 |
| 7 | 8 | 9 | 10 | 11 | 12 | 13 |
| 14 | 15 | 16 | 17 | 18 | 19 | 20 |
| 21 | 22 | 23 | 24 | 25 | 26 | 27 |
| 28 | 29 | 30 | 31 | | | |

| November | | | | | | |
|---|---|---|---|---|---|---|
| | | | 1 | 2 | 3 | |
| 4 | 5 | 6 | 7 | 8 | 9 | 10 |
| 11 | 12 | 13 | 14 | 15 | 16 | 17 |
| 18 | 19 | 20 | 21 | 22 | 23 | 24 |
| 25 | 26 | 27 | 28 | 29 | 30 | |

| December | | | | | | |
|---|---|---|---|---|---|---|
| | | | | | | 1 |
| 2 | 3 | 4 | 5 | 6 | 7 | 8 |
| 9 | 10 | 11 | 12 | 13 | 14 | 15 |
| 16 | 17 | 18 | 19 | 20 | 21 | 22 |
| 23 | 24 | 25 | 26 | 27 | 28 | 29 |
| 30 | 31 | | | | | |

*Dates to Remember*

# Goals For 2000-2001

Academic:

Personal:

Spiritual:

Social:

Physical:

Civic:

114

| Sunday | Monday | Tuesday | Wednesday | Thursday | Friday | Saturday |
|--------|--------|---------|-----------|----------|--------|----------|
|        |        |         |           |          |        |          |
|        |        |         |           |          |        |          |
|        |        |         |           |          |        |          |
|        |        |         |           |          |        |          |
|        |        |         |           |          |        |          |

# Goals For the Month of _____

Academic:

Personal:

Spiritual:

Social:

Physical:

Civic:

# Graduation Requirements

A student must earn 19 credits in grades 9, 10, 11, and 12 to graduate from high school. One credit equals one year or 180 (50 minute) hours of class work; one-half credit equals one-half year or 90 (50 minute) hours of class work; and one-quarter credit equals one-fourth year or 45 (50 minute) hours of class work. A school year is usually calculated as 36 weeks of daily 50 minute classes. Most high school textbooks are designed to equal a school year's worth of work. But be cautious and check the teacher's manual as some books are designed for half-year or two- year programs.

If you are taking classes at a college or university to apply to both high school and college (See Project Running Start), five quarter or three semester hour credits equal one high school credit.

**Minimum High School Graduation Requirements**

The following is the list of required courses for graduation in the state of Washington. If you live in another state you may want to check with your superintendent of public instructions for the exact requirements for your state.

The minimum state requirements are less restrictive than most individual private schools or public school systems. Most private and public high schools require 21 or 22 credits to graduate.

| Subject | Credits |
|---|---|
| English | 3 |
| Math | 2 |
| Science | 2 |
| Social Studies | 2.5 |
| State History & Government | .5 |
| U.S. History | 1 |
| Contemporary World History, Geography & Problems | 1 |
| Occupational Education | 1 |
| Health & Physical Education | 2 |
| Fine Arts | 1 |
| Electives | 5.5 |
| TOTAL | 19 credits |

## Course Content Requirements

The following are brief explanations of the required content for courses to qualify for high-school credit. Mathematics is not detailed as it is self-explanatory.

**English (Language Arts):** Three credits are required and may be satisfied by any combination of Literature, grammar, composition (including specific courses such as creative writing or report writing), spelling, vocabulary, and library-study skills. Most standard high-school English texts include a combination of grammar, composition, spelling, vocabulary, and library skills. Literature courses are usually contained in separate texts and usually include writing and vocabulary activities.

**Science:** Two credits are required, at least one of which is a lab science. For a course to qualify for a laboratory science, the student should be involved with experimentation, investigations, observation and the study and practice of the skills used by scientists. Simply studying the textbook and taking the tests does not meet the laboratory science requirements.

**Occupational Education:** This includes, but is not limited to, homemaking, industrial arts, business and office occupations, trade and industrial education. Courses such as 'Time Management' are considered Occupational Education - do not forget to give yourself credit for working through your guide book.

Some students choose to earn this credit through work experience and by maintaining a journal of work experience. A Work Experience credit requires supervision by a teacher, being past your sixteenth birthday, legal employment (may be volunteer, if your work does not displace a paid employee), employer provided reports of student's work record. You must include at least four hundred five (405) hours or more of work experience related to your school program. (Work experience credits may be applied to elective requirements or to occupational education requirement. A student may not earn more than one work experience credit.)

**Social Studies Requirements for Washington High School Students:**

One credit is required in United States history and government which shall include study of the Constitution of the United States. No other course content may be substituted as an equivalency for this requirement.

One-half credit shall be required in Washington State history and government which shall include the study of the Constitution of the State of Washington. (the Washington state history and government course requirement may be fulfilled by students in grades seven or eight or both. Credits earned in grades seven or eight shall not be applied toward the minimum number of credits required from high school graduation.

One credit shall be required in contemporary world history, geography, and problems. Courses in economics, sociology, civics, political science, international relations, or related courses with emphasis on current problems may be accepted as equivalencies.

**Physical Education/Health:** The two credit physical education/health requirement shall be met by course work in the areas of personal fitness development, leisure activities, health education/life skills management, and healthful living program.

**Fine Arts:** Fine Arts classes include drama, art, and music. Classes may be practical or appreciative in nature at the student's or teacher's discretion.

**Electives:** Courses that are selected to meet college admission requirements or to satisfy interests of the students. To satisfy minimum high school requirements for Washington State, you need at least five and a half (5.5) elective credits.

# TENTATIVE HIGH SCHOOL PLAN

Use Pencil to Complete

| | 9th | 10th |
|---|---|---|
| English | | |
| Mathematics | | |
| Social Studies | | |
| Science | | |
| Health and Physical Education | | |
| Occupational Education | | |
| Fine Arts Credit | | |
| Foreign Language | | |
| Electives | | |

# TENTATIVE HIGH SCHOOL PLAN
## Use Pencil to Complete

| 11th | 12th |
|------|------|
|      |      |
|      |      |
|      |      |
|      |      |
|      |      |
|      |      |
|      |      |
|      |      |
|      |      |
|      |      |
|      |      |
|      |      |
|      |      |
|      |      |
|      |      |
|      |      |
|      |      |
|      |      |
|      |      |
|      |      |
|      |      |
|      |      |
|      |      |
|      |      |
|      |      |
|      |      |
|      |      |
|      |      |
|      |      |
|      |      |
|      |      |
|      |      |
|      |      |
|      |      |
|      |      |
|      |      |
|      |      |
|      |      |
|      |      |
|      |      |
|      |      |

English

Mathematics

Social Studies

Science

Health and
Physical Education

Occupational
Education

Fine Arts Credit

Foreign Language

Electives

# Four Year College Entrance Recommendations

If your future plans include attending college, select a school program carefully. Planning should include meeting the admission requirements at the colleges of your choice, as well as meeting school graduation requirements.

Washington state supported colleges and universities require a minimum grade point average and/or SAT score. Private and out-of-state college entrance requirements vary and should be checked by the student as soon as he considers it likely he will attend that college.

| Subject | Recommendations |
|---|---|
| English | 4 years, college prep, honors or AP recommended |
| Math | Algebra, Geometry, Trigonometry, and Pre-Calculus |
| Science | Two years lab science required |
| | Biology, Chemistry, and physics recommended |
| Foreign Language | 2 years required; 3 or 4 years recommended |
| Social Studies | 3 years |
| Occupational Ed. | 1 year |
| Health/P.E. | 2 years |
| Fine Arts | 1 year |
| Academic Elective | 1 year minimum |

## Suggested Course Schedules For College-Prep Students

### Freshmen (9th)

English
Algebra
Foreign Language
Washington History(1/2 year)
P.E./Health
Earth Science
Elective (1/2 year)

### Sophomores (10th)

English
Geometry
Foreign Language
World History or elective
P.E./Health
Biological Science

### Junior (11th)

English
Algebra II with Trigonometry
United States History
Foreign Language
Chemistry or Physics
Occupational Education

### Senior (12th)

A.P. or Honors English
Pre-Calculus/Calculus
Contemporary World Problems/Civics
Foreign Language (Advanced)
Chemistry or Physics
Fine Art

# Freshman Year Plan

(Use Pencil to Complete)

| | 9th |
|---|---|
| English | |
| Mathematics | |
| Social Studies | |
| Science | |
| Health and Physical Education | |
| Occupational Education | |
| Fine Arts Credit | |
| Foreign Language | |
| Electives | |

# Checklist for 9th Grade

The following activities should be done during 9th grade (about age 14). Review this list before beginning your 10th grade year. Check off each item as it is completed

## All students

☐ I have completed a tentative course plan for grades 9 through 12.
☐ I have fulfilled all course requirements for my grade 9 course plan.
☐ I have participated in career exploration activities.
☐ I have participated in educational opportunity exploration activities.

## For College-bound students:

☐ I have chosen and completed at least four academic courses that are appropriate for my career goal. For example, a major in engineering generally requires four years of college preparatory math and science.

# Sophomore Year Plan
(Use Pencil to Complete)

| | 10th |
|---|---|
| English | |
| Mathematics | |
| Social Studies | |
| Science | |
| Health and Physical Education | |
| Occupational Education | |
| Fine Arts Credit | |
| Foreign Language | |
| Electives | |
| | |
| | |

# Checklist for 10th Grade

The following activities should be done during 10th grade (about age 15). review this list before beginning your 11th grade year. Check off each item as it is completed.

## All Students:

☐ I have reviewed my educational planning sheet and adjusted it as necessary. I have completed a tentative plan for courses in grades 10 through 12.

☐ I have fulfilled all course requirements for my grade 9 and 10 course plan.

☐ I have selected a tentative occupational goal.

☐ I have received or researched educational and/or career planning information necessary as preparation for 11th grade planning.

☐ I have fulfilled all course requirements for courses which I have chosen or made arrangements to make-up any deficiencies during the summer or during my 11th grade year.

## For College-Bound Students:

☐ I am enrolled in at least four academic courses that are appropriate to my career goals.

☐ I have begun researching tentative colleges and major fields of study.

☐ I have researched early college entry programs and/or Advanced Placement Testing opportunities.

## Vocational/job training:

☐ I have researched the prerequisite courses for my chosen field.

☐ I have researched my educational options, including half-day, high-school vocational programs in my chosen field.

☐ I am aware of the cost of the vocational training for my chosen career, and have researched scholarship/work-study options for this training.

# Junior Year Plan

(Use Pencil to Complete)

| | 11th |
|---|---|
| **English** | |
| **Mathematics** | |
| **Social Studies** | |
| **Science** | |
| **Health and Physical Education** | |
| **Occupational Education** | |
| **Fine Arts Credit** | |
| **Foreign Language** | |
| **Electives** | |
| | |
| | |

# Checklist for 11th Grade

The following activities should be done during the 11th grade (about 16 years old). Review this list before beginning your 11th grade courses and check off each appropriate item as it is completed.

## For All students:

☐ I have reviewed my educational planning sheet and adjusted it as necessary. I have completed a tentative plan for courses in grades 11-12.

☐ I have fulfilled all course requirements for my grade 9, 10, and 11 course plan.

☐ I have selected a tentative occupational goal.

## For College-bound Students:

☐ I am taking sufficient number of academic subjects appropriate to my career goal.

☐ I have enrolled in a course or arranged to study for the Advanced Placement tests I plan to take this year.

☐ I have scheduled the test dates for the Advanced Placement exams I plan to take this year.

☐ I have enrolled in a early college entry program.

☐ I have researched information on colleges, scholarships, and financial aid and I have begun the process of selecting a college.

☐ I have signed up in September or early October to take the PSAT (Preliminary Scholastic Aptitude Test).

☐ I have registered to take the Washington Pre-College Test in the spring.

☐ I have begun the nomination process for the military academies of my choice.

☐ I have narrowed and refined my college choices.

## For Students Planning Vocational/job training:

☐ I have researched my educational options for attending a community college program, vocational school or apprenticeship program.

☐ I am aware that some post-high school vocational programs require up to a two-year waiting time. I have followed the required procedures to get on the waiting list.

# Senior Year Plan

(Use Pencil to Complete)

| | 12th |
|---|---|
| **English** | |
| **Mathematics** | |
| **Social Studies** | |
| **Science** | |
| **Health and Physical Education** | |
| **Occupational Education** | |
| **Fine Arts Credit** | |
| **Foreign Language** | |
| **Electives** | |

# Checklist for 12th Grade

The following activities should be done during 12th grade (about age 17). Twelfth grade career planning activities should be started as early as possible during the fall. This planning is extremely important, especially for the college-bound student. Review this list when you register for courses and check when completed.

## For All Students:

☐ I have reviewed and checked my planning sheet.

☐ I have reviewed the credits I have earned toward graduation. I have made arrangements to make-up any deficiencies that exist.

☐ I have visited with a career counselor for help in selecting a career or vocation.

☐ I have met with recruiters from all branches of the military service. (For students considering military careers.)

☐ I have applied for graduation, and ordered my cap and gown.

## For College-bound Students:

☐ I have checked admission requirements for my choice of colleges.

☐ I have taken the college entrance exam(s) WPC, ACT, or SAT in the early fall (if not taken last spring).

☐ I have reviewed my college choices for the final selection and application and have written for out-of-state college application forms and procedures.

☐ I have made application to the college or colleges of my choice early this fall.

☐ I have made plans to attend the appropriate college information sessions.

☐ I have applied for financial aid during the month of January.

☐ I have applied for scholarships at national, state, and local levels.

☐ I have arranged to study for and take the exams for Advanced Placement Programs which will benefit me.

☐ I have researched and enrolled in appropriate early-entry college courses.

## For Students Planning Vocational/Job training:

☐ I have made application to the community college or vocational school **as soon as it was possible.**

☐ I applied for financial aid during the month of January.

☐ I applied for scholarships.

☐ I am aware of the fee schedules and possible financial aid available for the school(s) I am considering.

☐ I am aware that some post-high school vocational programs require up to a two-year waiting time. I have followed the required procedures including paying the fees to get on the waiting list of the school(s) I am interested in.

# Course Planning Sheet

Name of Course: _____

Number of Credits: _____ Credit Category: _____

Date to Start: _____ Finish Date: _____

Brief Description: _____

_____

_____

_____

_____

Overall Purpose/Aim: _____

_____

_____

_____

_____

Specific Learning Objectives: _____

_____

_____

_____

_____

_____

_____

_____

_____

_____

# Resources and Materials

Reference Materials:

Books and Magazines:

Other Media:

Outside and Ongoing Activities:

People:

Places:

130

© 1996, 1994, 1992 by Beverly L. Adams-Gordon

# Course Requirement Sheet

Name: _____

Course Name: _____ Ref #: _____

| Order to be Completed | Project, Report or Assignment | Due Date | Est. Time Required | Date Started | Date Com-pleted | Pts Earned __ of __ |
|---|---|---|---|---|---|---|
| | | | | | | |
| | | | | | | |
| | | | | | | |
| | | | | | | |
| | | | | | | |
| | | | | | | |
| | | | | | | |
| | | | | | | |
| | | | | | | |
| | | | | | | |
| | | | | | | |
| | | | | | | |
| | | | | | | |
| | | | | | | |
| | | | | | | |
| | | | | | | |
| | | | | | | |
| | | | | | | |

| Order to be Completed | Project, Report or Assignment | Due Date | Est. Time Required | Date Started | Date Com- pleted | Pts Earned of |
|---|---|---|---|---|---|---|
| | | | | | | |
| | | | | | | |
| | | | | | | |
| | | | | | | |
| | | | | | | |
| | | | | | | |
| | | | | | | |
| | | | | | | |
| | | | | | | |
| | | | | | | |
| | | | | | | |
| | | | | | | |
| | | | | | | |
| | | | | | | |
| | | | | | | |
| | | | | | | |
| | | | | | | |
| | | | | | | |
| | | | | | | |
| | | | | | | |
| | | | | | | |
| | | | | | | |
| | | | | | | |
| | | | | | | |
| | | | | | | |

# Project-Report Grading Form

Name: _____     Date Completed: _____

Subject: _____     Report Number: _____

---

**Research Quality**
60 Possible Points/ 60% of Grade
12-10 Superior; 9-7 Excellent; 6-4 Good; 3-1 Fair

Historical accurate/authentic; no serious omissions: _____

Grasp of subject/topic in context: _____

Provides analysis of data not just a description: _____

Used at least 2 sources(not including encyclopedia):
    Annotated bibliography for each reference. _____

Balanced presentation & different viewpoints taken into account;
    Critical use of sources: _____

**A: Total Points Research Quality:** _____

---

**Quality of Presentation**
20 Possible Points/ 20% of Grade
4 Superior; 3 Excellent; 2 Good; 1 Fair

Organization of written material (follows Guidelines): _____

Grammar/Spelling/Punctuation: _____

Creative/original view of topic: _____

Props/costumes/illustrations/display accurate: _____

Construction of Time Line (no serious omissions/visual appeal): _____

**B: Total Points Quality of Presentation:** _____

---

**Oral Report/Discussion with teacher**
20 possible points/ 20% of Grade
5-4 Superior; 3 Excellent; 2 Good; 1 Fair

Demonstrates knowledge of cause & effect relating to topic: _____

Demonstrates grasp of individual events & their significance: _____

Able to express ideas articulately: _____

Demonstrates familiarity with resources cited: _____

**C: Total Points for Interview:** _____

---

**Total Score (A+B+C):** _____

Reports receiving less than 30 points will not be accepted.
You must go back and improve on weak areas

# Project Report Writing Guidelines

**Form of Report:**
    1) Title Page
    2) Introduction with thesis statement.
    3) Actual Report
    5) Conclusion: Logically follows from thesis statement & body.
    6) Footnotes/Endnotes: numbered consecutively; proper form/placement.
    7) Supplemental materials (illustrations, maps, charts, etc.)
    8) Bibliography:
        a) Must use at least two references, not including encyclopedia
        b) Annotated bibliography is required for each reference.
        c) Written in proper form on separate page.

**Mechanics:**
    1) Ink, not pencil, and/or typed.
    2) If typed, it must have 1 inch margins on all sides.
    3) Pages must be consecutively numbered.
    4) One side of the page only.
    5) If typed, it must be double spaced.
    6) BE NEAT - BE NEAT!
    7) Style:
        a) no abbreviations
        b) no contractions
        c) watch your grammar, capitalization, punctuation & spelling
        d) Literary style - should fit your topic - here are some ideas:
            1) point of view of imaginary person who could have lived during this time
            2) Factual person: as a diary or journal from their point of view
            3) a chronological account with all the interesting facts
            4) may be a script for a play, etc.

# Timeline or Project:

    1) All reports must have a timeline; neatly done, illustrated with pictures, appropriate scale, most important events dated and described, etc.
    2) In lieu of a timeline, you may include other project ideas such as:
        a) Create a game on the topic.

        b) Demonstrate a skill related to your research, i.e. if you are researching Foods of the 17th Century, you could prepare a meal composed of those foods (or reasonable substitutes).

        c) Write a song which expresses the facts.

        d) Create a decorama (e.g. of typical southern plantation, etc.)

        e) Create a bulletin board display or large poster which describes the facts.

# Essay and Composition Grading Form

Name: _____ Date Completed: _____

Subject: _____ Report Number: _____

Assignment topics and dates

| Content | 1 | 2 | 3 | 4 | 5 | 6 | 7 | 8 | 9 |
|---|---|---|---|---|---|---|---|---|---|
| Addresses the purpose of the assignment | | | | | | | | | |
| Exhibits a sense of audience | | | | | | | | | |
| Keeps to the topic | | | | | | | | | |
| Expresses originality and/or imagination | | | | | | | | | |
| Demonstrates clear ideas | | | | | | | | | |
| Uses specific details and examples | | | | | | | | | |
| Employs effective and appropriate language | | | | | | | | | |
| Includes a variety of sentence patterns | | | | | | | | | |
| **Organization** | | | | | | | | | |
| States main idea in a clear topic sentence | | | | | | | | | |
| Evokes interest in opening sentence | | | | | | | | | |
| Includes supporting sentences relating to topic | | | | | | | | | |
| Uses effective transitions | | | | | | | | | |
| Provides a sense of closure in concluding sentence/paragraph | | | | | | | | | |
| **Usage and Mechanics** | | | | | | | | | |
| Uses complete sentence structure | | | | | | | | | |
| Follows conventions of English grammar | | | | | | | | | |
| Punctuates correctly | | | | | | | | | |
| Capitalizes correctly | | | | | | | | | |
| Exhibits neatness | | | | | | | | | |
| Spells accurately | | | | | | | | | |
| **Specific Criteria** (Character development or facts presented, etc.) | | | | | | | | | |
| | | | | | | | | | |
| | | | | | | | | | |
| | | | | | | | | | |

# Comments

**Strengths**

Assignment 1: _____
_____

Assignment 2: _____
_____

Assignment 3: _____
_____

Assignment 4: _____
_____

Assignment 5: _____
_____

Assignment 6: _____
_____

Assignment 7: _____
_____

Assignment 8: _____
_____

Assignment 9: _____
_____

**Weaknesses**

Assignment 1: _____
_____

Assignment 2: _____
_____

Assignment 3: _____
_____

Assignment 4: _____
_____

Assignment 5: _____
_____

Assignment 6: _____
_____

Assignment 7: _____
_____

Assignment 8: _____
_____

Assignment 9: _____
_____

# Project Plan Sheet

Project Name: _____

_____

Due Dates: _____ Review Dates: _____

Description of Assignment/Project (attach assignment sheet): _____

_____

_____

Purpose of Assignment/Project: _____

_____

_____

_____

Details and Tasks to be completed: _____

_____

_____

_____

_____

_____

_____

_____

_____

_____

_____

_____

# Project Schedule

Outline of Steps:

_____ / _____

_____ / _____

_____ / _____

# Priority Tasks This Week

| Priority Rating | Scheduled | Description | Completed |
|---|---|---|---|
|  |  |  |  |
|  |  |  |  |
|  |  |  |  |
|  |  |  |  |
|  |  |  |  |
|  |  |  |  |
|  |  |  |  |
|  |  |  |  |
|  |  |  |  |
|  |  |  |  |
|  |  |  |  |
|  |  |  |  |
|  |  |  |  |
|  |  |  |  |
|  |  |  |  |
|  |  |  |  |
|  |  |  |  |
|  |  |  |  |

| Monday | Tuesday | Wednesday | Thursday | Friday | Saturday |
|---|---|---|---|---|---|
|  |  |  |  |  | Sunday |

# Goals for the week of _____

Academic:

Personal:

Spiritual:

Social:

Physical:

Civic:

# Monday, _____    _____

| Time | | | Notes |
|---|---|---|---|
| 6:00 | | | |
| 6:30 | | | |
| 7:00 | | | |
| 7:30 | | | |
| 8:00 | | | |
| 8:30 | | | |
| 9:00 | | | |
| 9:30 | | | |
| 10:00 | | | |
| 10:30 | | | |
| 11:00 | | | |
| 11:30 | | | |
| 12 Noon | | | |
| 12:30 | | | |
| 1:00 | | | |
| 1:30 | | | |
| 2:00 | | | |
| 2:30 | | | |
| 3:00 | | | |
| 3:30 | | | |
| 4:00 | | | |
| 4:30 | | | |
| 5:00 | | | |
| 5:30 | | | |
| 6:00 | | | |
| 6:30 | | | |
| 7:00 | | | |
| 7:30 | | | |
| 8:00 | | | |
| 8:30 | | | |
| 9:00 | | | |

# Tuesday, _____

| Time | | | Notes |
|------|---|---|-------|
| 6:00 | | | |
| 6:30 | | | |
| 7:00 | | | |
| 7:30 | | | |
| 8:00 | | | |
| 8:30 | | | |
| 9:00 | | | |
| 9:30 | | | |
| 10:00 | | | |
| 10:30 | | | |
| 11:00 | | | |
| 11:30 | | | |
| 12 Noon | | | |
| 12:30 | | | |
| 1:00 | | | |
| 1:30 | | | |
| 2:00 | | | |
| 2:30 | | | |
| 3:00 | | | |
| 3:30 | | | |
| 4:00 | | | |
| 4:30 | | | |
| 5:00 | | | |
| 5:30 | | | |
| 6:00 | | | |
| 6:30 | | | |
| 7:00 | | | |
| 7:30 | | | |
| 8:00 | | | |
| 8:30 | | | |
| 9:00 | | | |

# Wednesday, _____ _____

| Time | | | Notes |
|---|---|---|---|
| 6:00 | | | |
| 6:30 | | | |
| 7:00 | | | |
| 7:30 | | | |
| 8:00 | | | |
| 8:30 | | | |
| 9:00 | | | |
| 9:30 | | | |
| 10:00 | | | |
| 10:30 | | | |
| 11:00 | | | |
| 11:30 | | | |
| 12 Noon | | | |
| 12:30 | | | |
| 1:00 | | | |
| 1:30 | | | |
| 2:00 | | | |
| 2:30 | | | |
| 3:00 | | | |
| 3:30 | | | |
| 4:00 | | | |
| 4:30 | | | |
| 5:00 | | | |
| 5:30 | | | |
| 6:00 | | | |
| 6:30 | | | |
| 7:00 | | | |
| 7:30 | | | |
| 8:00 | | | |
| 8:30 | | | |
| 9:00 | | | |

# Thursday, _____ _____

| | | | Notes |
|---|---|---|---|
| 6:00 | | | |
| 6:30 | | | |
| 7:00 | | | |
| 7:30 | | | |
| 8:00 | | | |
| 8:30 | | | |
| 9:00 | | | |
| 9:30 | | | |
| 10:00 | | | |
| 10:30 | | | |
| 11:00 | | | |
| 11:30 | | | |
| 12 Noon | | | |
| 12:30 | | | |
| 1:00 | | | |
| 1:30 | | | |
| 2:00 | | | |
| 2:30 | | | |
| 3:00 | | | |
| 3:30 | | | |
| 4:00 | | | |
| 4:30 | | | |
| 5:00 | | | |
| 5:30 | | | |
| 6:00 | | | |
| 6:30 | | | |
| 7:00 | | | |
| 7:30 | | | |
| 8:00 | | | |
| 8:30 | | | |
| 9:00 | | | |

# Friday, _____  _____

| | | |
|---|---|---|
| 6:00 | | |
| 6:30 | | |
| 7:00 | | |
| 7:30 | | |
| 8:00 | | |
| 8:30 | | |
| 9:00 | | |
| 9:30 | | |
| 10:00 | | |
| 10:30 | | |
| 11:00 | | |
| 11:30 | | |
| 12 Noon | | |
| 12:30 | | |
| 1:00 | | |
| 1:30 | | |
| 2:00 | | |
| 2:30 | | |
| 3:00 | | |
| 3:30 | | |
| 4:00 | | |
| 4:30 | | |
| 5:00 | | |
| 5:30 | | |
| 6:00 | | |
| 6:30 | | |
| 7:00 | | |
| 7:30 | | |
| 8:00 | | |
| 8:30 | | |
| 9:00 | | |

Notes

# Saturday, _____  _____

| | | | Notes |
|---|---|---|---|
| 6:00 | | | |
| 7:00 | | | |
| 8:00 | | | |
| 9:00 | | | |
| 10:00 | | | |
| 11:00 | | | |
| 12 Noon | | | |
| 1:00 | | | |
| 2:00 | | | |
| 3:00 | | | |
| 4:00 | | | |
| 5:00 | | | |
| 6:00 | | | |
| 7:00 | | | |

# Sunday, _____  _____

| | | | Notes |
|---|---|---|---|
| 6:00 | | | |
| 7:00 | | | |
| 8:00 | | | |
| 9:00 | | | |
| 10:00 | | | |
| 11:00 | | | |
| 12 Noon | | | |
| 1:00 | | | |
| 2:00 | | | |
| 3:00 | | | |
| 4:00 | | | |
| 5:00 | | | |
| 6:00 | | | |
| 7:00 | | | |

# Course Record #_____

Course: _____ Credits: _____ Grade: _____

Subject: _____ Date Begun: _____ Finished: _____

Course Description: _____

_____

_____

_____

_____

_____

Main Textbook /Resources Used: _____ Copyright Year: _____

Publisher: _____

ISBN: _____ Text Level: _____

Comments: _____

_____

_____

_____

Grading Method: _____

_____

_____

_____

_____

_____

Projects and Activities I participated in for this course: _____

_____

_____

_____

_____

_____

_____


What I gained from this course: _____

_____

_____

_____

_____

_____

_____

_____


Teacher Comments on Student's Progress: _____

_____

_____

_____

_____

_____

_____

_____

# Transcript/Report Card

Name: _____ Expected Graduation: _____

Address: _____

Parent/Legal Guardian: _____ Birthdate: _____

Gender: _____ Notes: _____

| Date Com-pleted | Subject | Course Description | Ref # | Attempted Credits | Credits Earned | Grade |
|---|---|---|---|---|---|---|
| | | | | | | |
| | | | | | | |
| | | | | | | |
| | | | | | | |
| | | | | | | |
| | | | | | | |
| | | | | | | |
| | | | | | | |
| | | | | | | |
| | | | | | | |
| | | | | | | |
| | | | | | | |
| | | | | | | |
| | | | | | | |
| | | | | | | |
| | | | | | | |
| | | | | | | |
| | | | | | | |
| | | | | | | |
| | | | | | | |
| | | | | | | |
| | | | | | | |
| | | | | | | |
| | | **End of Year Summary** | | | | |
| | | **To Date Summary** | | | | |

What I Learned and accomplished this year: _____

_____

_____

_____

_____

_____

_____

_____

_____

_____

Teacher/Parent Comments on Student's Progress: _____

_____

_____

_____

_____

_____

_____

_____

_____

_____

# Reading record

List books as you read them. You should list books read for pleasure as well as those read for your course work and projects.

Book title: _____

Author: _____

Publisher: _____ Copyright: _____ ISBN: _____

Describe briefly: _____

_____

_____

---

Book title: _____

Author: _____

Publisher: _____ Copyright: _____ ISBN: _____

Describe briefly: _____

_____

_____

---

Book title: _____

Author: _____

Publisher: _____ Copyright: _____ ISBN: _____

Describe briefly: _____

_____

_____

Book title: _____

Author: _____

Publisher: _____ Copyright: _____ ISBN: _____

Describe briefly: _____

_____

_____

_____

Book title: _____

Author: _____

Publisher: _____ Copyright: _____ ISBN: _____

Describe briefly: _____

_____

_____

_____

Book title: _____

Author: _____

Publisher: _____ Copyright: _____ ISBN: _____

Describe briefly: _____

_____

_____

_____

# Experience Record Summary

Name: _____

| Date Completed | Experience Record Title/Summary | Reference Number |
|---|---|---|
| | | |
| | | |
| | | |
| | | |
| | | |
| | | |
| | | |
| | | |
| | | |
| | | |
| | | |
| | | |
| | | |
| | | |
| | | |
| | | |
| | | |
| | | |
| | | |
| | | |
| | | |
| | | |

| Date Completed | Experience Record Title/Summary | Reference Number |
|---|---|---|
| | | |
| | | |
| | | |
| | | |
| | | |
| | | |
| | | |
| | | |
| | | |
| | | |
| | | |
| | | |
| | | |
| | | |
| | | |
| | | |
| | | |
| | | |
| | | |
| | | |
| | | |
| | | |
| | | |
| | | |

# Experience Record

Name: _____

Activity: _____

Date Begun: _____ Date Ended: _____

Where: _____

    Supervisor: _____

    Address: _____

    City, State, Zipcode: _____

    Phone Number: (_____)_____

Description of Activity: _____

_____

_____

_____

_____

_____

_____

_____

_____

_____

_____

_____

_____

_____

_____

# Experience Record

Name: _____

Activity: _____

Date Begun: _____ Date Ended: _____

Where: _____

   Supervisor: _____

   Address: _____

   City, State, Zipcode: _____

   Phone Number: (_____)_____

Description of Activity: _____

_____

_____

_____

_____

_____

_____

_____

_____

_____

_____

_____

_____

# Scholarships Earned

## (Store Documents in Safe Deposit Box or Metal File Cabinet)

| Date | Title | Purpose | Value |
|------|-------|---------|-------|
|  |  |  |  |
|  |  |  |  |
|  |  |  |  |
|  |  |  |  |
|  |  |  |  |
|  |  |  |  |
|  |  |  |  |
|  |  |  |  |
|  |  |  |  |
|  |  |  |  |
|  |  |  |  |
|  |  |  |  |
|  |  |  |  |
|  |  |  |  |
|  |  |  |  |
|  |  |  |  |
|  |  |  |  |
|  |  |  |  |

# College Savings Bond List

### (Store Savings Bonds in Safe Deposit Box or Metal File Cabinet)

| Face Value | Serial Number | Purchase Date | Maturity Date | Redeemed (Date) |
|---|---|---|---|---|
|  |  |  |  |  |
|  |  |  |  |  |
|  |  |  |  |  |
|  |  |  |  |  |
|  |  |  |  |  |
|  |  |  |  |  |
|  |  |  |  |  |
|  |  |  |  |  |
|  |  |  |  |  |
|  |  |  |  |  |
|  |  |  |  |  |
|  |  |  |  |  |
|  |  |  |  |  |
|  |  |  |  |  |
|  |  |  |  |  |
|  |  |  |  |  |
|  |  |  |  |  |
|  |  |  |  |  |

**Income and Expenses for \_\_\_/\_\_\_**

| Date | Description | Income | Expense | Charity | Savings | School | Clothing | Entertain-ment | Miscel-laneous |
|------|-------------|--------|---------|---------|---------|--------|----------|----------------|----------------|
| | | | | | | | | | |
| | | | | | | | | | |
| | | | | | | | | | |
| | | | | | | | | | |
| | | | | | | | | | |
| | | | | | | | | | |
| | | | | | | | | | |
| | | | | | | | | | |
| | | | | | | | | | |
| | | | | | | | | | |
| | | | | | | | | | |
| Monthly Total | | | | | | | | | |

# Financial Summary for _____

| Month | Income | Expense | Description of Expenses | | | | | |
|---|---|---|---|---|---|---|---|---|
| | | | Charity | Savings | School | Clothing | Entertain-ment | Miscel-laneous |
| January | | | | | | | | |
| February | | | | | | | | |
| March | | | | | | | | |
| April | | | | | | | | |
| May | | | | | | | | |
| June | | | | | | | | |
| July | | | | | | | | |
| August | | | | | | | | |
| September | | | | | | | | |
| October | | | | | | | | |
| November | | | | | | | | |
| December | | | | | | | | |
| 19__ Totals | | | | | | | | |

# Index

# Books Published By
# Castlemoyle Books

### Spelling Power by Beverly L. Adams-Gordon

A comprehensive spelling program which requires just 15 minutes per day. Extensive resource materials include: word lists organized by phonetic principles and spelling rules with six levels of built-in review, alphabetical list of the 12,000 most frequently used words, over 134 hands-on games and activities, placement and diagnostic tests and complete step-by-step instructions. Instructions for teaching proofreading and dictionary skills are also covered. The only spelling book you will ever need for ages 8 to adult. 1-888827-05-X  $49.95

### Spelling Power Activity Task Cards

365 Cards used to assign instructional activities for the Spelling Power program. 280 of these activities are not duplicated in the Spelling Power manual. All activities provide solid education in a fun, hands-on way. Teacher's guide provides index of activities and complete directions. Use to supplement Spelling Power or other spelling programs. 1-888827-10-6   $24.95

### Spelling Power Quick Start Video, Vol. 1

After a short presentation of what research has proven to be the most effective instructional procedures, you will be guided step-by-step through the key aspects of the Spelling Power program. After watching this 90-minute video-seminar you will be able to start using the Spelling Power prgram with little or no advanced preparation. 1-888827-11-4    $24.95

### Spelling Power Quick Start Video, Vol. 2

This video provides details and demonstrations on how teachers can incorporate individualized and hands-on learning activities into their spelling instruction. Explains how to teach using multi-sensory, inductive, and deductive approaches. To be released Fall 1996. 1-888827-12-2  $24.95

### Spelling Power Quick Start Video, Vol. 3

The third video in the Quick Start Video Series will focus on teaching the Integrated Functional Writing activities discussed in Chapter 3 of Spelling Power. You will learn about motivating students to write, teaching proofreading skills, and integrating writing with spelling and other curriculum areas. To be released Winter 1997. 1-888827-13-0    $24.95

### Home School, High School, and Beyond by Beverly L. Adams-Gordon

A course designed to help home schooled teens take a more active, thoughful role in their education. Teens and their parents are guided in collecting, organizing, and maintaining high school home schooling records in preparation for college or other post-high school education and career. 1-888827-15-7 $17. 95

### Recipes For Fun! by Jo Berg

This collection of 68 arts and craft recipes will give you the answer for what to do when there is nothing to do!  While many of the recipes are "old favorites," you will find some pretty unusual activities too. Recipes include everything from sidewalk chalk to dog biscuits. 1-888827-16-5      $6.95

**Available From Your Favorite Educational Supplier or**
**Castlemoyle Books**
**15436 42nd Avenue South**
**Seattle, WA. 98188**
**206/439-0248**
**1-888-SPELLTOO (toll free)**
**or Visit our Web Site at www.seanet.com/~jgordon**
Please add 10% of total for Shipping and handling or $5. whichever is greater.
Prices subject to change after Jan. 1, 1997.